From *Nutshell News Magazine*

AF830657

KIT RENDERINGS

Ron Benson

Mrs. Carol Pelowsky
2503 Woodside Dr.
Cross Plains, WI 53528-9506

KALMBACH BOOKS

Contents

Introduction

THE *QUEEN ANNE* period of furniture design extends far beyond the years of her reign, 1701–1714. Early furniture is identified by the use of the *cyma* curve, an elongated "s" curve. Early tables and chairs have little carving, depending upon burl walnut veneer and elegant lines for their beauty. Before the introduction of mahogany in 1720 most furniture was executed in walnut. In America cherry was also popular.

During this era there were many new types of tables such as tea tables and gaming tables. The dining room table disappeared; this followed French fashion, in which dining in small groups replaced large public meals of the court.

Case pieces, chests of drawers, for example, were straight-lined and plain. Decoration varied from plain burl veneer to elaborate oystering, marquetry, and painted decoration in the Chinese manner. The highboy, developed in the William and Mary period, reached perfection in this era.

Chairs were the best of Queen Anne design. Chair makers eliminated stretchers while creating some of the strongest chairs ever produced. After 1720 the plain lines began to elaborate as the advantages of mahogany for carving altered the previous simplicity.

Thomas *Chippendale* was the first designer to lend his name to a style, thanks to his publication of three successful books of designs from 1754 to 1762. His designs used mahogany, a strong and easy-to-carve wood. Chippendale designs mixed baroque and rococo details. Lines were generally straighter than in the previous style, but an increase in carving gave an impression of complexity.

There were few new furniture forms in this style. The tripod table, which was used for so many things—tea tables, for example—was one of few genuinely new innovations. During this period the collecting of china became almost a mania. New pieces were produced to display these collections: hanging shelves, brackets, and the china cabinet were but a few.

Chests of drawers came in a wide variety, from straight-lined chests with ogee (curved) bracket feet to serpentine fronts. These shaped chests required the use of veneer but only in small amounts. English chests used more veneer than American.

Seating furniture remained most important. Chairs became more highly carved. Cabriole legs slowly were replaced by the straight "Chinese" leg. Chinese and gothic influences in the legs and backs flattened out the curved lines of the earlier baroque-rococo. One interesting change was the return of stretchers, done for visual balance rather than structural rigidity.

Hepplewhite furniture was the first popular neoclassical style. It was a middle-class Adam style. There were many new pieces. The most noticeable change was the return of dining rooms and with them sideboards and dining tables. Hepplewhite used much less carving than previously, relying instead on delicate inlays and beautiful satinwood veneers. He used light woods and pastel paints to reverse the dark palette of earlier furniture. Mahogany continued to be popular but was considered provincial.

Some of the earlier Hepplewhite furniture also followed later French rococo lines, particularly chests of drawers and small tables. These pieces, while inlaid and veneered, rarely had any carving.

Sheraton is often called the finest of the period designers. His first book of drawings was beautifully illustrated. It had exact drawings of some Robert Adam pieces and showed rooms from the extravagant homes of the prince regent, later George IV.

Sheraton returned to a dark palette, but continued to use some satinwood. He is especially noted for the use of ebony and black and dark green paint. Many neoclassical details were painted in realistic colors on his designs.

His chairs returned turnings to popularity and modified ancient Greek chair designs. He introduced the récamier, often used in reverse pairs. Many of his designs had secret compartments with hidden springs to open a section. He designed chairs that turned into library steps and—his best idea—used leaves to extend the size of dining tables.

Classical designs were influenced by the archeological discoveries of ancient Pompeii and Napoleon's attempt to identify France with ancient Rome. Lines and details became simplified in an almost modern way. In France beautiful mahogany veneers decorated flat surfaces that were then set off with ormolu attachments. All designs were rather boxy, including the seats of chairs.

By 1820 the simplicity of early Classical designs had become a seeking for novelty, especially in America. By 1840 the early elegance of Classical had become so debased that the complexities of Victorian design must have seemed a welcome relief.

Ron Benson

High Style

Create an elegant highboy with just a few modifications

Craftmark's #40022 or 40023 highboy kit is probably the most striking furniture kit on the market. Whether you build it as #40022, with a straight top, or as #40023 the bonnet topped highboy, you're sure to end up with a showpiece. Unfortunately, as with many kits today, it is flawed by a lack of attention to authentic detail. Our alterations will correct most of the problems and open up new possibilities.

The kit you will be working with is slightly different from the photograph. Craftmark has altered the drawer details for the better so that the lip you see on my photo of the drawers has been eliminated; otherwise we will be working with the same kit.

MATERIALS

- Craftmark's #40022 or 40023 Chippendale highboy kit
- Midwest basswood 1/8" thick
- Midwest basswood 1/32" thick
- Very small double molding
- Water based paint
- Testor's gold paint
- X-Acto knife
- Glue
- Craftmark's walnut stain or "glaze" stain

This kit is remarkably easy to assemble. I suggest you do the entire kit *without glue* to get a feel for what alterations need to be done. Besides my obvious changes you will probably need to sand down the drawers a bit to get them to fit properly. Eliminate the columns, parts #6 and 7. They are not correct and we don't need them anyway. Part #15, the top, will need to be shortened to fit flush in the front (see drawing). This is necessary because without the columns it is too deep. Make a new base for the top using 1/8" basswood. It should be the same size as the bottom of the kit top.

With the drawer fronts you have three choices. The least authentic choice is to use the fronts as they are and sand the bevel down a bit so that it isn't so high. This will look all right, but genuine Queen Anne highboys (despite the kit name, this is *not* a Chippendale piece) with beveled drawer fronts would have the fronts overlapping the openings. In fact, this is your second choice. Reverse the beveled edge so that it faces *inside*. The fronts of the drawers are now flat and will have new fronts glued on. Place the fronts down on a piece of flat 1/32" basswood. With a pencil or pen trace around each drawer (see drawing). Each of these tracings will be slightly larger than the drawer fronts provided in the kit. Use a steel edge ruler or template to cut out each of these new fronts. Drawer #7 on the drawer guide will have the lower lip flush with the drawer bottom; drawer #8 will have the top lip flush (see drawing). This is because both fit flush against the molding. The straight topped version will have the three top drawers with the lip flush to the top because we will be putting molding directly above these three drawers. With a fine grade sandpaper, round the lip of each drawer to give the impression of a very slight bevel. Our final option is only for the straight topped highboy since it is a detail too early for bonnet tops. As previously, reverse the drawer fronts so that the fronts are flat. Glue a double bead molding around each drawer *opening*. Do *not* glue these on the drawers; that technique is much too late for Queen Anne. The top drawers and #7 and 8 will have a molding around only three sides. This is authentic (see drawing for detail).

Drawer #10 with the shell will look best if the shell stands out. If you use the molding around the drawer openings this front will have to be reversed. The shell motif is too late for molding around the openings, so you really have only two options with this drawer. First sand the front down a bit so that the bevel is very slight and the shell projects. You may need to add a stop (small piece of wood) behind the drawer to make it flush with the other drawers. Second, add a small molding to the outside edge of the drawer, then sand it down (see drawing). This too will require a stop or you will knock off

the molding when you close the drawer.

This kit has unusually fine legs. You will need to alter the feet, but except for cutting down the curve on the back legs, the legs are excellent. The back legs need to be softened at the knee (see drawing). The four legs on a genuine highboy are *not* identical. The back legs are slightly flatter. If this were not the case these huge pieces would sit even farther out into the room. This is never obvious, except on country pieces, so keep it subtle.

I have chosen to do a slipper foot. I believe this is easier than a pad foot, but both are similar. Experiment with the rear legs first so that if you make a mistake the worst will be behind and you can put your best feet forward.

The feet have a pad underneath and the "slipper foot" just above. With an X-Acto knife slightly cut around the foot about 1/16" from the bottom. This is a guide line for your needle file. File lightly around the line until it looks similar to mine. With a pencil draw a point on each foot and file to this point (see drawing).

The only other alterations are the two backs, #56 and #62. Score a couple of horizontal lines on the larger back. This will simulate genuine backs with a couple of pieces of wood instead of the single pieces shown in the kit. It is best

---

*This beautiful highboy (**opposite, top**) will accent any room. Several of the slight changes can be seen with the legs (**opposite, bottom**) and back (**above, right**) of the piece.*

to do this freehand since the antique boards would have been cut by hand.

The basic lines of the bonnet top are good, but I have included an alteration which is much finer (see drawing).

You need to stain the back, underside and top with Craftmark's walnut or "glaze" stain. This includes the bonnet top. You may paint your highboy black, dark green, red or yellow. Those are the correct period colors in the order in which they were the most popular. I used ordinary Testor's gold paint.

For early japanning (the gold on lacquer) the figures were raised in slight relief. I suggest you simply paint the gold directly on the color and leave it flat.

My painting is freehand, but I don't expect every reader to be able to paint such intricate designs without help. There is a delightful way to cheat — photocopiers! Check out a good book on period furniture with pieces similar to ours. Select front views and copy them. You may have to set the machine to lighter or darker so you can see the design clearly. If it isn't the same size you want, set the machine to enlarge or reduce the image. It may take some playing about to get the exact size you want, but once you get it, there are two things you can do to shortcut freehand talent. First, cut out each drawer from the photocopy, pin the corners lightly (see drawing) until it is centered on the drawer. Now take a needle and lightly punch around the entire design. You will probably want to omit some of the fussier detail. When you lift the paper you will have the design in tiny pinpricks on the drawer front. You can now paint the drawer the color you want and the pinpricks will still show through. These will be your guide for the "freehand" drawing of the detail. Fill the pinpricks with just a drop of gold paint before you paint the entire design. It's just like "fill in the dots," only smaller. Use a very fine brush and don't worry if you slip up — it's only paint. If you make a mistake, paint over it. Avoid the temptation to make up your own design. Unless you are very familiar with period design, you will probably make a mistake. I had to copy parts from two original japanned highboys to get my ideas for this piece, and I have a very strong background in period design. This is an area where originality is not an advantage.

Your drawerpulls fit directly over the painting! Some figures will get covered up, but that is authentic.

You may find that when you have done all of the above that you are happy enough with the results to stop there (I did). For those who want

DIAGRAMS FOR HIGHBOY

SIDE VIEW

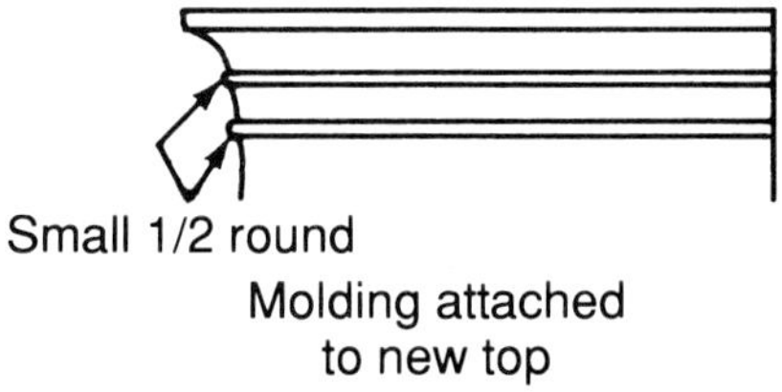

to go that extra mile, add a final clear finish. If this is to be an antique, remember that these were valuable pieces which were well treated. Wear and tear will be at a minimum. Confine your antiquing to wiping the "glaze" stain over the clear finish, and wipe nearly all of it off.

There you have it. If you made the bonnet topped highboy, you have a miniature of a piece which would bring over a quarter of a million dollars — that should be worth all that extra minute work!

DIAGRAMS FOR HIGHBOY

DRAWER DETAIL

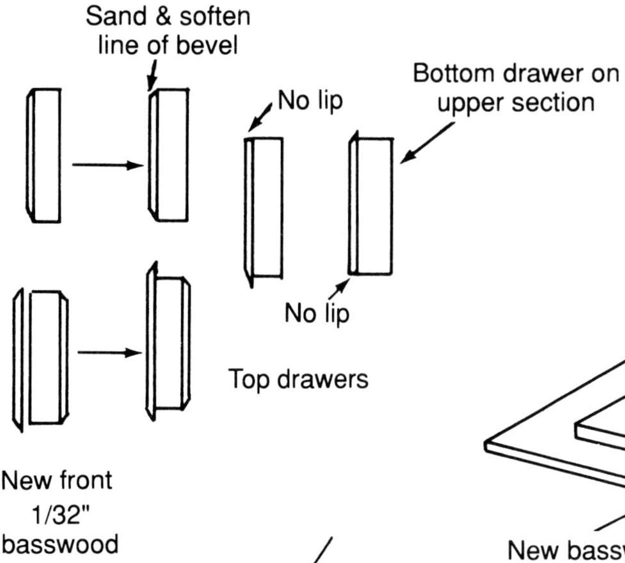

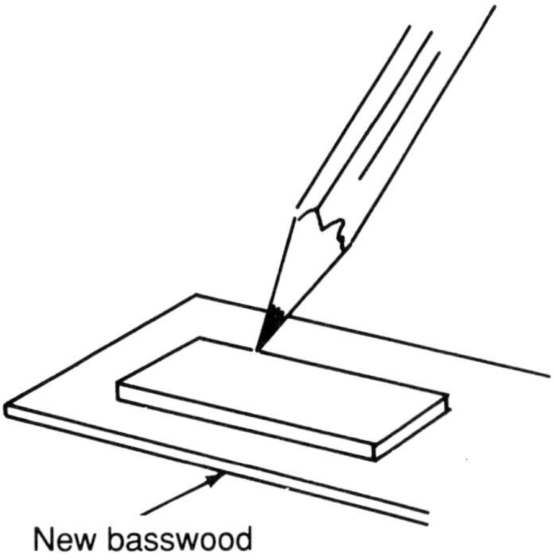

Trace drawer fronts

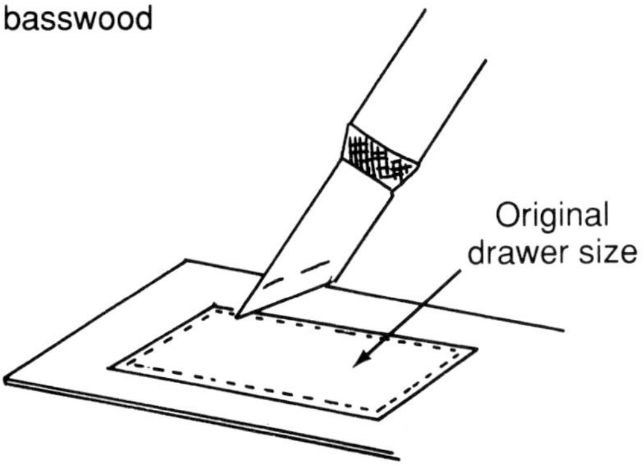

Cut out new
drawer fronts

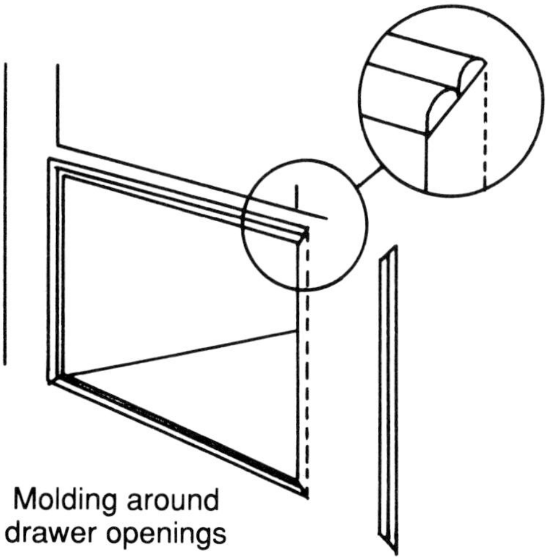

Molding around
drawer openings

DIAGRAMS FOR HIGHBOY

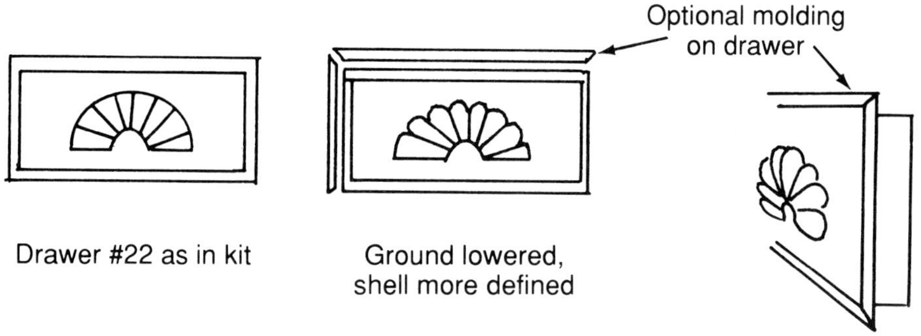

LEG

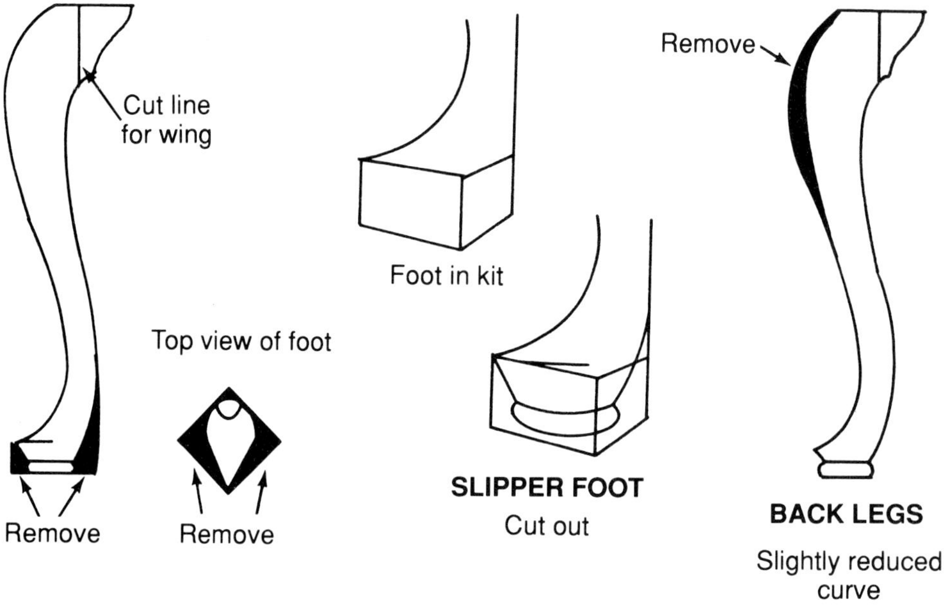

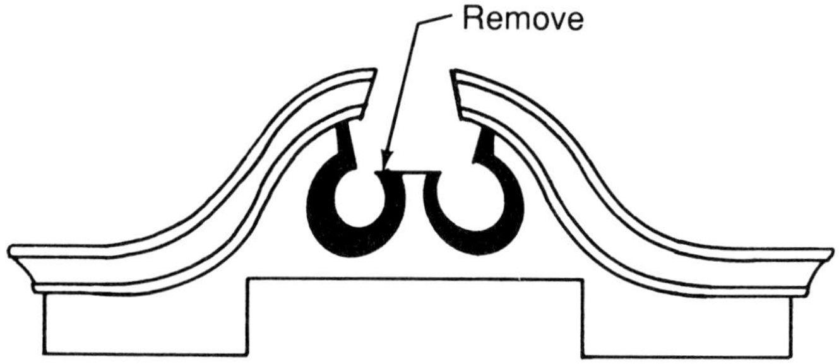

BONNET TOP OPTION

DIAGRAMS FOR HIGHBOY

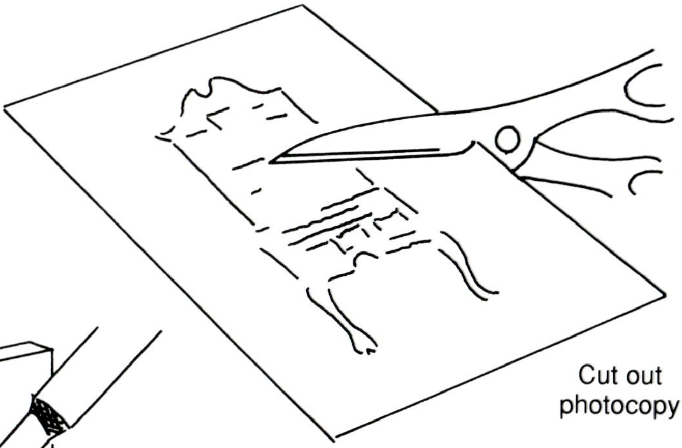

Cut out photocopy

BACKS

Score backs to simulate smaller boards

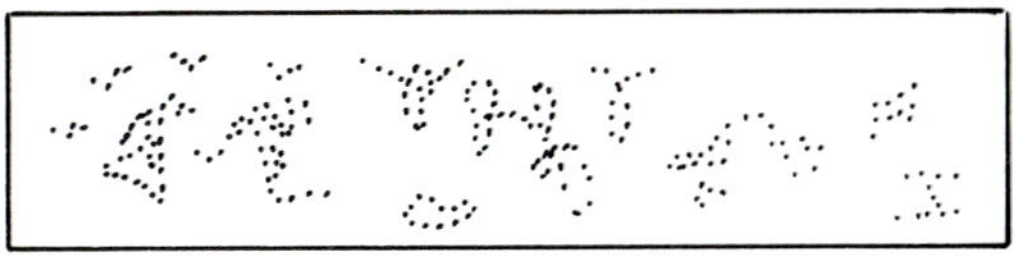

Design in pin pricks

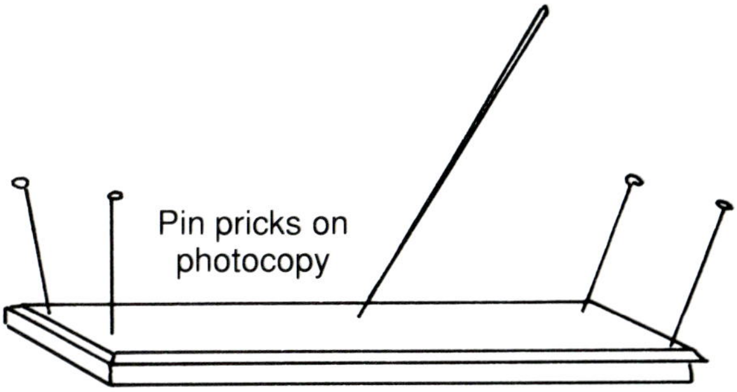

To the Queen's Taste

Queen Anne tea table serves with elegance

WHEN TEA DRINKING became an everyday activity early in the 18th century on both sides of the Atlantic, many articles appeared for serving it properly, and special tables were made for displaying the tea service. Queen Anne tea tables were round or rectangular, with the narrow rim of the dished top safely confining the tea service. The rim resulted from carving down the top, leaving a raised edge.

Craftmark's #40039 Queen Anne tea table contains all the elements of a really fine piece of furniture, and it is relatively simple to assemble and convert.

INSTRUCTIONS

Before you assemble the apron, Parts 1 and 0, use my template to reshape it. I have given it a graceful scallop. Be sure the end curve doesn't come too close to the edge. It should meet the top of the legs. Cut one side, then use it as a template for the other side (see drawing).

Next, reshape the side apron, Part 1. Use my template to cut the shape, then use the newly cut part to cut and match the other side (see drawing).

I cut these designs using an X-Acto knife and sandpaper rolled up on a round pencil. The sharp crease was done with a small file and a piece of folded sandpaper. If you happen to own a small scroll saw, you may cut the design with it. I have included an alternate design specifically for this saw; it is more particularly American and should not be painted. These were usually produced in walnut.

Now glue Parts 0, 1, and 99 (the top) together as shown in the kit instructions. Let these parts dry, then round the corners slightly, leaving the upper edge square (see drawing). You will not be using Part 2, the quarter-round outside molding.

The legs are the next parts to improve. I chose to make slipper feet, but you may prefer the more traditional pad feet. The drawings illustrate both.

Whichever you choose, the legs, Part 6, have very generous feet — too generous. Remove the excess wood as shown in the drawing. Check the photographs and drawings to get a feel of the proportions. Note that a good deal of wood is removed from the back, as well as the front of the foot.

I suggest a "pad" under either type of foot. The pad is an example of good quality, but it also acts as a guide when you cut the foot. It ensures that each foot will be the same height and be cut the same amount. If you have a good eye, make your foot without it, but lower the top of the foot so that it doesn't look too

MATERIALS

- #40039 Craftmark Queen Anne Tea Table
- Dark green water based paint
- Jamestown Colony Red by Minicolor
- Small natural sponge (optional)
- Water based gold paint
- White glue
- X-Acto knife
- Calendar pictures (optional)
- Ivory water based paint (optional)
- Small file
- Sandpaper

chunky (see drawing).

Note how I rounded the knee and front of the leg. The back of the leg is only slightly rounded and retains its square feeling.

If you are going to stain your table, cut a line at the top of the legs to indicate the wings (see drawing). You may add this to your painted version as well, but the line may not show.

Now miter and glue the top molding in place as suggested in the kit instructions. Once the top is dry, take a paper clip and run it back and forth against the grain, as shown in my drawing. This will give the slight uneven effect of 18th century planes and help to make the grain a bit tighter for a smoother finish on the top. Don't overdo this. Antiques were not obviously handmade. Craftsmen of the time tried to get them as perfect as possible.

Glue the legs into place, making sure they don't set in from the edge. You may need to round them a bit to ensure a smooth join.

Before you begin painting, stain the underside with Craftmark's walnut stain. This will make it look as if it has some age. If you intend to stain the entire piece, use a 50-50 mix of Craftmark's walnut and mahogany stain. This will look like American walnut. You can get a burl effect by sponging the stain on the apron. The stain should be put on rather dry (see drawing). Test this on an extra piece of wood. Use a natural sponge, one of the very small ones found in art supply shops.

You have several choices of color. The most popular colors were Chinese red, black, green, mustard yellow, and, on very fancy pieces, ivory. Except for red and ivory, any color may be used without decoration. These two colors were expensive and used only on very fine pieces.

Paint the entire piece in your choice of color, then scrape a little off to indicate wear. If you are using decoration, remember the finer pieces were well taken care of and will have less wear. Notice that my table has only slight wear on the lower legs and the rim, but is otherwise in good condition.

I used a dark green water based paint that was finished with Craftmark's clear coat. Then I painted gold over that, and covered the gold with clear finish. If you use enamel, give the raw wood a clear finish before you paint the color. Be sure you let each stage dry thoroughly before you proceed to the next.

I based my Chinoiserie decoration on an English Queen Anne grandfather clock ca. 1705. I took the leg designs from a set of chairs of the same date. At this early date, figures and flowers were painted over gesso (hard plaster) decorations to give them relief. This should not be used on the top, where only flat decoration was used. Tea sets would have chipped gesso in no time. You can "draw" your flowers and figures with white glue on a toothpick, as I did. Let it dry, and then go over it a couple of times to build it up. In the photographs you can see that the raised decoration is rather limited.

While I painted most of my decoration freehand, there are some easy ways to aid painting. For the top, I cut the corner angles from a piece of manila folder and used it as a template for the corners (see drawing). Paint the corners with long black rectangles. Also paint a "mountain" in black in the center of the top. Use the drawing as a guide. These form the background for the gold Chinoiserie decoration. I used water based gold paint by Deka that I bought at an art supply shop. The advantage of water based paint is that it dries faster and cleanup is easier. Use my drawings or copy a photograph of Chinoiserie designs you like from a book. Reduce them until you get a useful size. Take the designs you have selected and place them on your table. Use a pin to lightly prick the design on the paper into the wood below. This will be your guide for the gold lines. Now all you

Diagrams

Kit Renderings

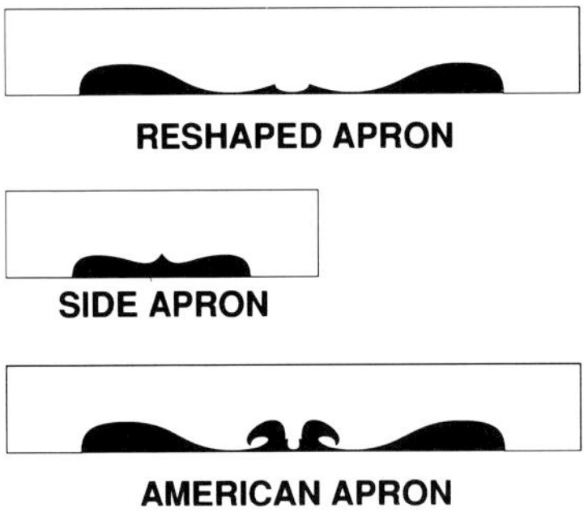

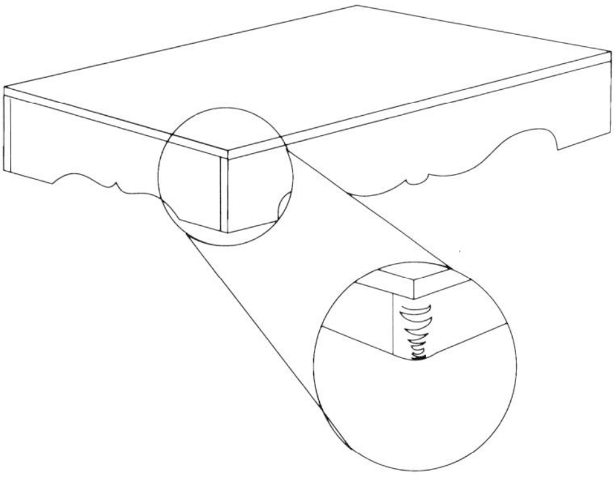

round apron corners, keeping top square

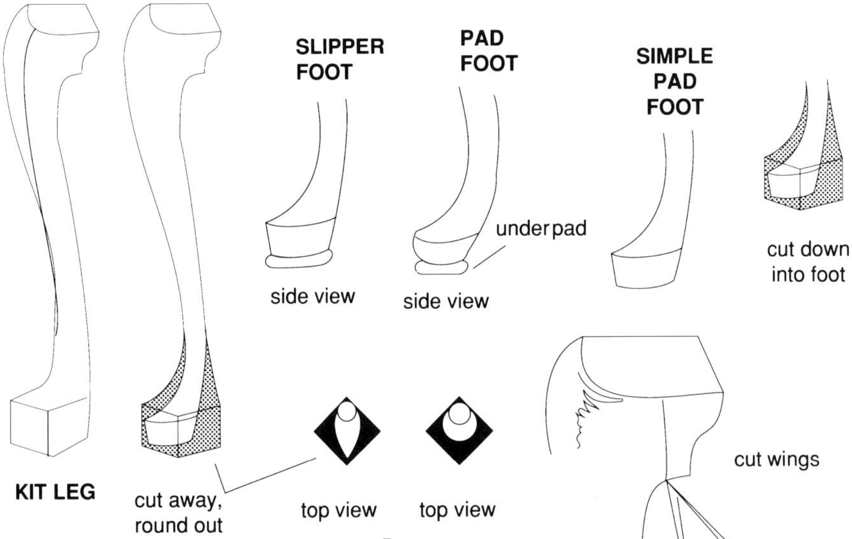

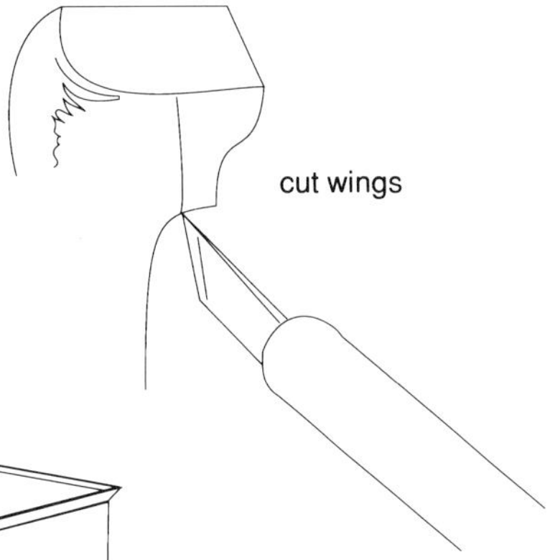

cut wings

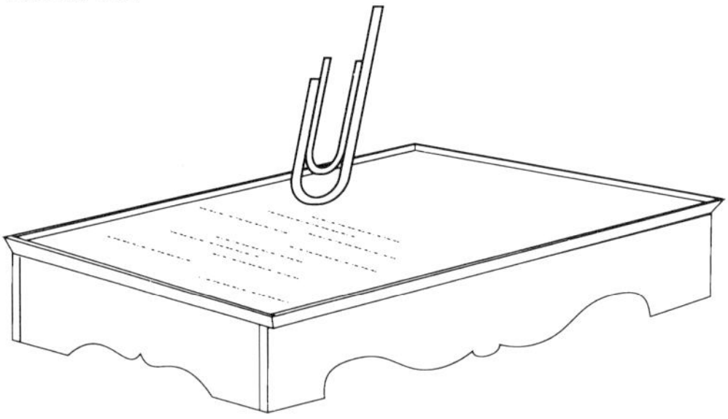

use paper clip to simulate antique plane marks

Diagrams

Kit Renderigs

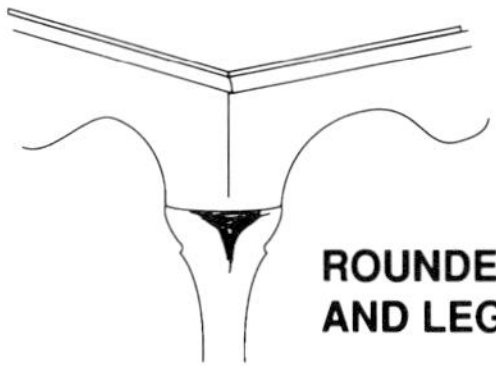

ROUNDED CORNER AND LEG

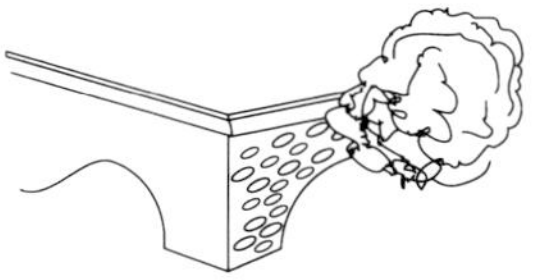

BURL EFFECT WITH NATURAL SPONGE

MANILA TEMPLATE FOR CORNERS
paint corners black

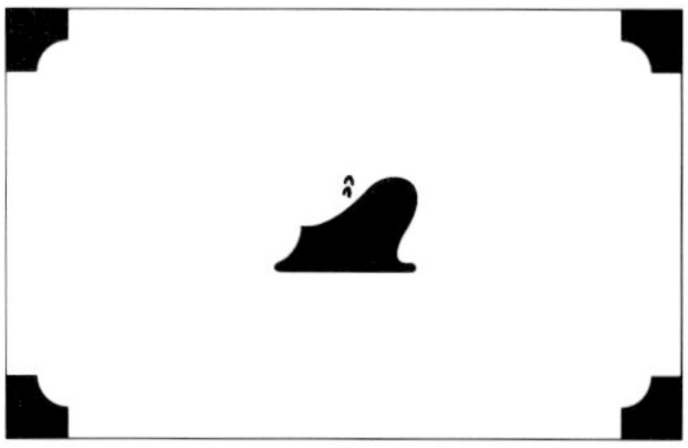

BLACK AREAS ON TOP

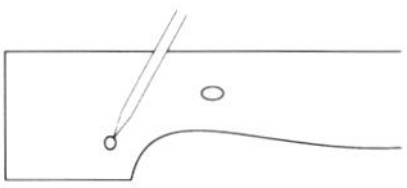

use drops of glue to build
up flowers and figures

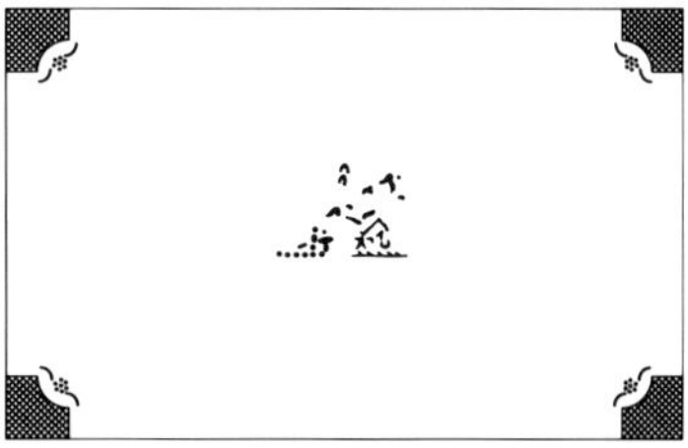

GILT DESIGN
shown without black

CHINOISERIE DECORATION ON SIDES

CORNERS

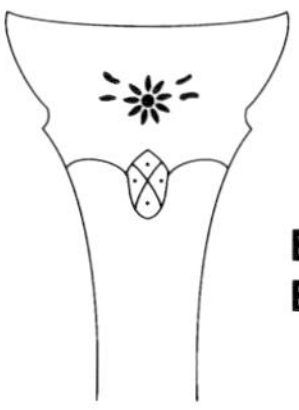

BLACK BACKGROUND

KNEE SHOWING TYPICAL DETAIL

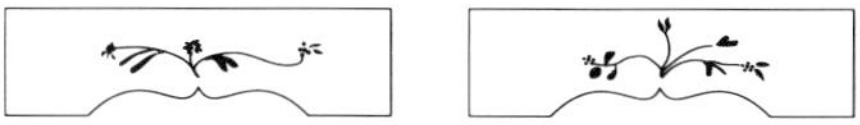

CHINOISERIE DECORATION ON ENDS

Diagrams

FRENCH INSPIRED TABLE

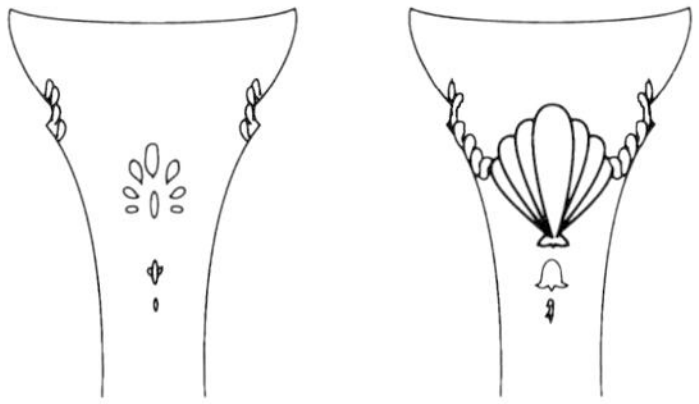

GLUE DETAIL **GOLD DETAIL**

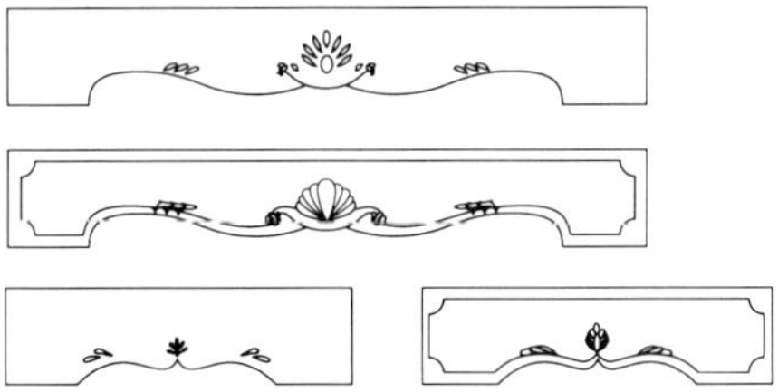

APRONS WITH RAISED GLUE DETAIL

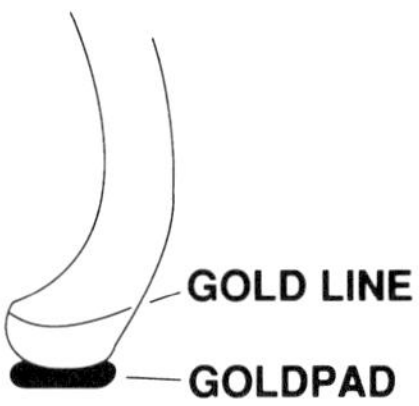

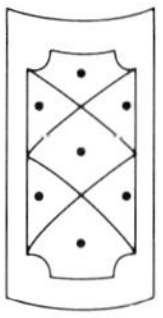

CORNER DETAIL FLAT GOLD OVER WHITE

need do is connect the dots with gold paint and you have your decoration.

After I painted the gold, I touched up the inside of the flowers with Minicolor Jamestown Colony Red. This makes them stand out, and it looks authentic, too.

The ivory table can be done in the French manner instead of Chinese. I cut out the overdoor frames from above the doors in the French room on the cover of the 1992 NUTSHELL NEWS Miniatures calendar. The paintings are *exactly* the size of the table top. Glue them in place and paint the table ivory to match. I have included an entirely different design for this version (see drawings). This design is symmetrical. Build up the shells with glue, and paint the gold over them. Paint the gold over the top as well, so that all of your gold matches.

There you have it — two wonderful choices in several finishes. Whichever you choose, you will have one of the prizes among antiques. These tables are rarely under $24,000 and frequently run as high as $100,000! Not bad for a do-it-yourself job!

Fit for a Queen

Turn this Chippendale chair into a royal style

THE SCROLL ARMED wing chair is one of the most desirable antiques. Originally these chairs were used in bedrooms where the wings protected readers from drafts. Many had brass swing-arm candlesticks attached to the wings. Most of these have disappeared over the years. Today, scroll armed wing chairs are used mostly in living rooms, despite the fact that the wings make conversation difficult from the side.

Craftmark's #40016 Chippendale style wing chair is a wonderful jumping off point for a fine Queen Anne or Chippendale wing chair.

INSTRUCTIONS

We will start at the bottom. The kit comes with a very straight seat when viewed from the top (parts #52 and #55). The rear sections need to angle as shown in the drawing. These parts are also not wide enough in front. Note on the drawing that I have added two new end pieces, just over 1/8" each, to each part and slightly rounded the front ends. You need also to remove a small amount vertically from each side of the back, part #51. This should match the amount you have removed from the seat parts.

The two sides with wings, parts #53 and #54, have a very awkward and overly generous wing. Remove the excess wood as seen in the drawing. To be sure they match, complete one

MATERIALS

- Craftmark #40016 Chippendale wing chair
- Small scraps of basswood
- X-Acto knife
- One set Craftmark #43111 small cabriole legs
- Velverette glue
- Cotton ball
- Manila paper
- Chrome ring from ballpoint
- Craftmark mahogany stain kit
- Craftmark walnut stain (optional)

side and use it as a template for the other side.

The scroll arms, parts #59, should be cut at a vertical angle (see drawing). This makes the top of the arm larger than the bottom. The reverse side will be exactly the opposite. Reshape the arm so that from the top view it will look almost as if it is a circle joined onto the arm (see drawing and photograph). Set these aside to upholster later.

Before we begin our legs, let's start the upholstery. I took a few short cuts which actually make the chair look more authentic. Begin with the foam back, part #57. I cut it smaller and angled the top (see drawing) to make a gentle roll for the top. Keep the back thin. Heavy padding is a mark of a reproduction or modern upholstery. Upholster as suggested in the drawings. Glue the fabric over the back, wrapping your fabric as seen in the drawing. Do not allow much excess fabric. You need only a small amount to hold it properly.

Next we will upholster the arms. I glued the upholstery with Velverette glue. If you are careful, it is possible to glue upholstery directly to parts that show. Test your fabric first. Some fabrics will always have to be glued at out-of-sight locations. I put a *thin* coating of glue at the back of the fabric I intended to use for the top edge of the arms. When this dried, I glued and cut it onto parts #53 and #54. Only a tiny amount overlaps the edges. This will be covered and will not show.

The cushion in this top view reflects the changes made in the seat, with tapered rear and widened front. Tops of wings and arms were upholstered with pieces carefully cut to shape. The wings have been cut back for a lighter look.

The upper part of the arms and wing fronts were upholstered by the above method. When my glue dried on the fabric back, I cut it to shape, using the re-cut template which is provided in the kit, and glued it directly on top of the arm and wing front. Some fabrics, like velvet, may require that you glue the fabric to the template before you glue it onto the arm. Should you need to do this, cut your template even smaller so that the fabric does not bulge over the arm.

You need upholster only the front of part #52, our re-worked seat base. The rear will be covered by the cushion. My fabric had a selvage edge which did not need to be cut or glued under. This is an advantage since you can glue your legs directly to the wooden underside, which makes for a strong join.

The cushion, part #55, needs two alterations. First, cut the same angle out of the rear of the foam seat (part #56) as you cut from parts #52 and #55. Don't add anything to the foam. The edge should round and not thick. Before upholstering, add some cotton from a cotton ball to give some additional height and rounding. Upholster this by gluing the fabric from the bottom as shown in the drawing. Note that the cushion does not show a seam in the front. This is the typical 18th century manner. The seat does not look like a soft box.

Now glue all these parts together as shown in the drawing. The last thing to do is to cut a thin piece of manila paper for the back. Use my template as a guide. When you wrap the upholstery around this paper, it will be too thick at the edges and bulge out a bit. To correct this, cut two or more (depending on the thickness of your fabric) pieces of manila paper to fill in the back and give a smooth fit (see drawing). When

The Chippendale style leg has simulated wings, carved knee, and claw and ball foot surmounted with a carved ring. Typical of the 18th century, the front of the cushion does not have a seam. The photograph has been enlarged to show detail.

this is finished, you may glue the back into place. All of your upholstery is now finished.

Our major alteration is the legs. For some reason this kit comes with straight legs, which were never used with the scroll arm. You have two choices — you may make Chippendale legs as I have done, or you may make Queen Anne legs. Whichever you choose, begin with Craftmark's #43111 small cabriole legs.

Shortly we will chop out a section of these legs, but follow these instructions first: Cut two small vertical slits on each leg to simulate the wings which are separate pieces of wood on genuine chairs (see drawing). This shell knee is easy to make. Use the chrome ring from a ballpoint for the entire shell. Lightly sketch the shell onto the knees. Push the chrome ring into the drawn lines. In my drawing, note how I get the side detail of the shell. Our lovely "carved" detail is done with a penny! I sketched where I wanted indentation, then pushed the penny into these lines. Since the shell will be lightly sanded and antiqued, the pencil lines will not show.

Our claw and ball is also created with a chrome ring bent into an oval and pushed into all four sides of each foot. I deepened the ball by scraping an X-Acto knife along this detail (see drawing). You also need to notch the back of the leg to give an authentic line to the foot (see drawing).

When the legs are finished, cut 1/4" from each leg, just slightly above the foot. Round the two remaining parts so that the upper part is slightly larger than the lower. With your X-Acto knife, lightly score a line just above the cut on the upper part (see drawing). Use a file to shape this line into a collar, or ring. When the two match and look as if they are one leg, glue them together. I set these into the corners of the kit box to dry and to keep them level and straight. The collared leg is fairly common on antiques, but is not often reproduced, therefore many of you may not be familiar with it. It was popular in England.

Our Queen Anne legs are also created from Craftmark's #43111 legs. This time we will not cut anything from the middle. Cut the upper 1/8" off just above the notch. Round the entire upper knee and cut "wings" into it as shown for the Chippendale leg.

The foot is a bit more complicated. As you can see in the drawing, a great deal is removed vertically. Do this before you cut the bottom off. Then sand the foot into a slender tube shape. Then remove 1/8" from the foot. This gives you your Queen Anne foot in the right size, but with some small details to add and remove. Cut the rear of the foot in a notch as shown, then angle the entire foot. Voila! A wonderful Queen Anne leg and pad foot. It is a tiny bit skinny, but certainly within acceptable standards.

The back legs, parts #60 and #28, are cut narrower so that there are no notches for a stretcher. I also thinned the lower part of the legs a bit (see photograph).

Our Chippendale chair should have mahogany stain on the legs. The Queen Anne would be best with a 50/50 mix of Craftmark's Mahogany and Walnut stain. Do *not* use the walnut by itself; it's far too dark. Finish either with Craftmark's clear sealer, then antique with their "glaze" finish.

Our chair would have been English c. 1740-50. The Queen Anne version would have been 30 years earlier. Either of these would happily grace any room you choose to place it in.

Diagrams

Kit Renderings

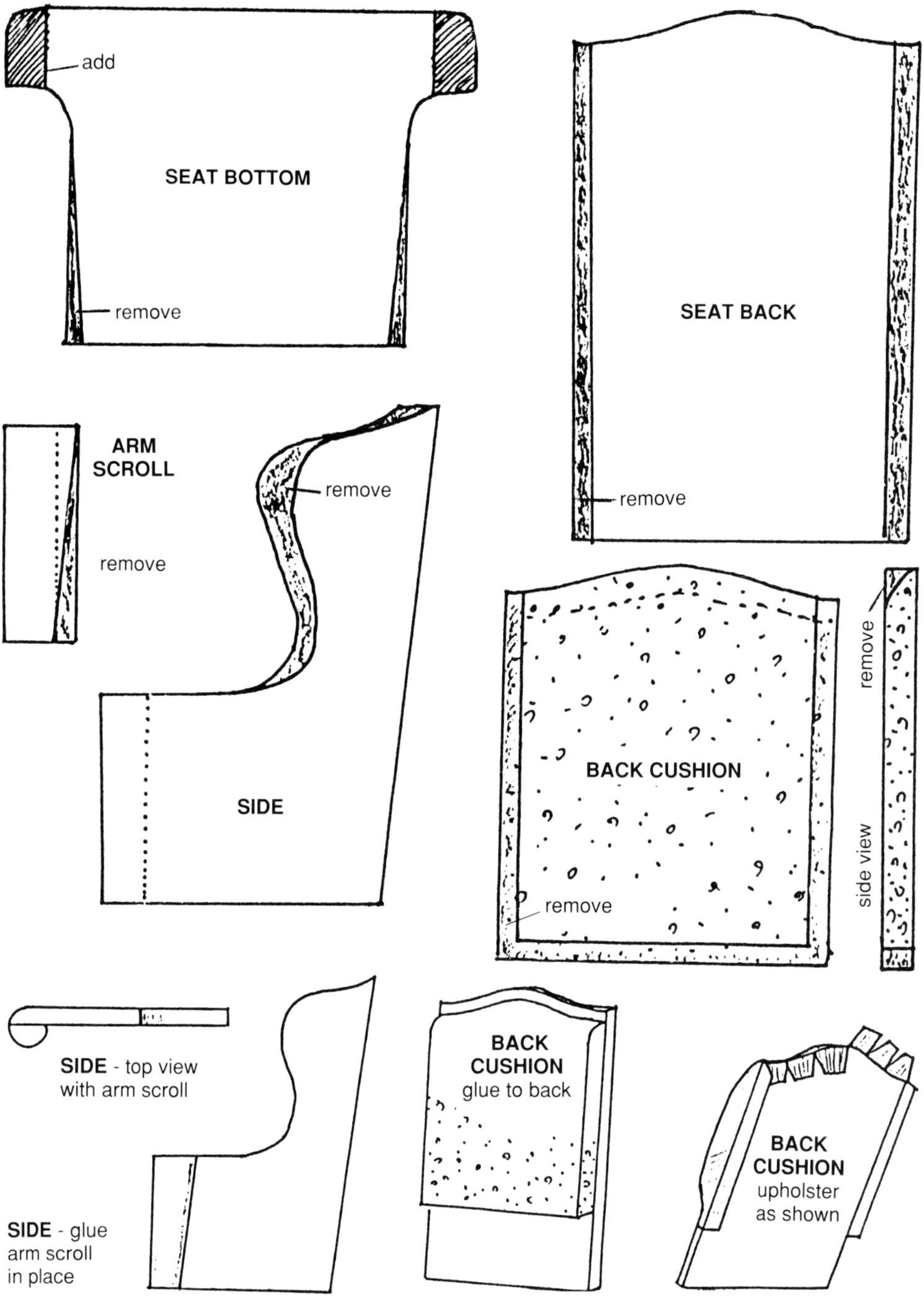

Diagrams

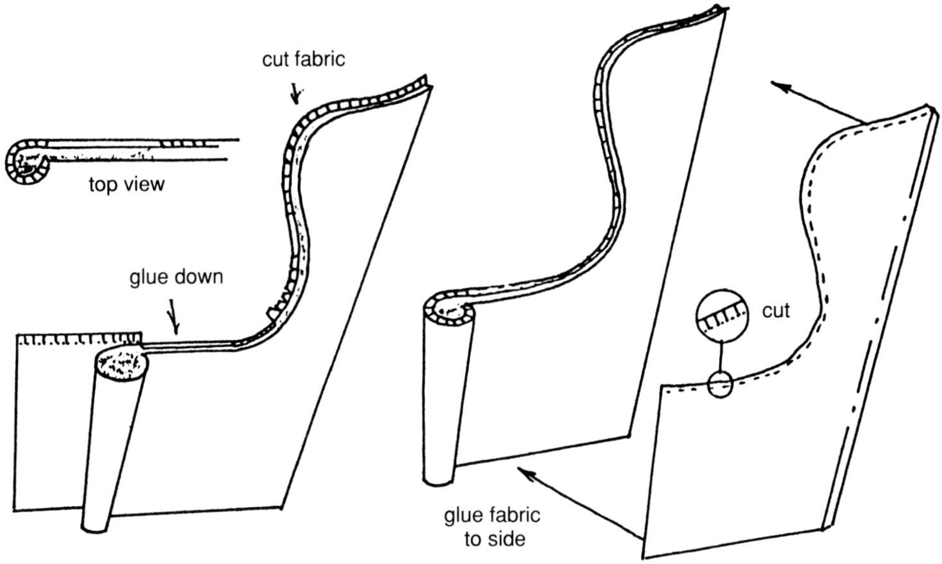

PART 52 UPHOLSTERY

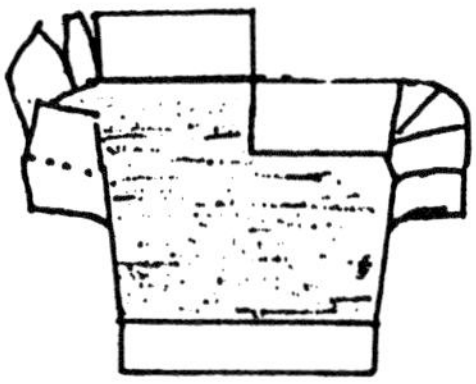

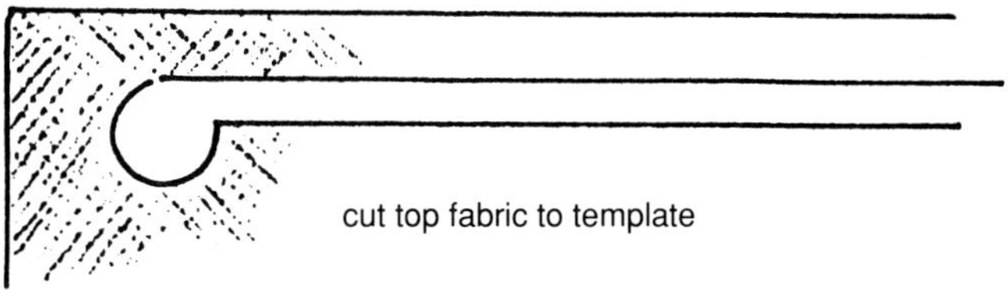

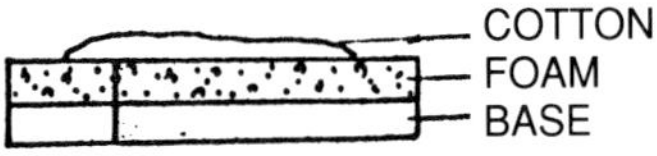

PART 55 - side view

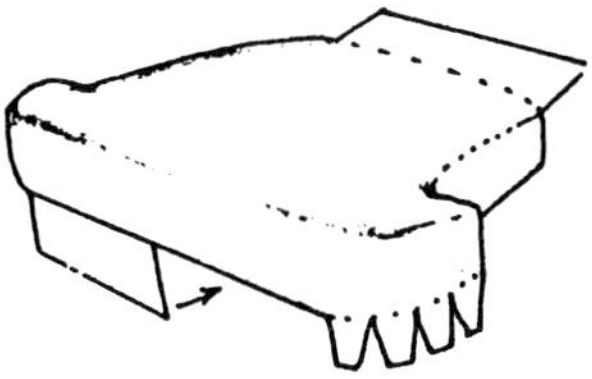

PART 55 UPHOLSTERY

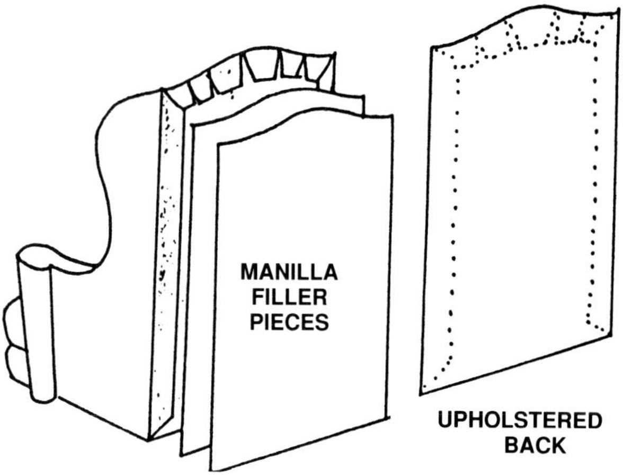

Diagrams

SHELL ON KNEE

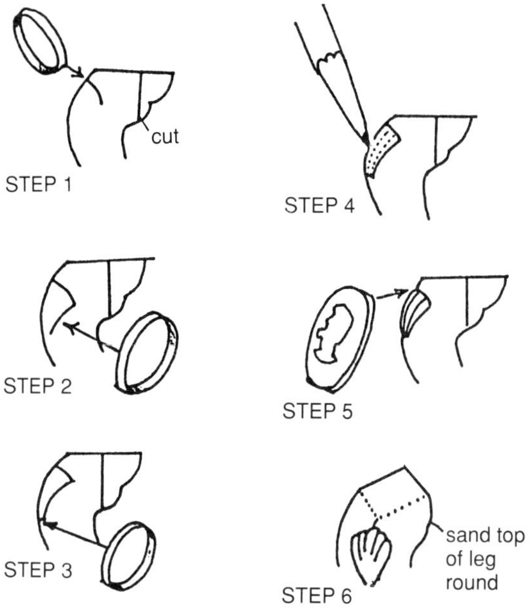

CLAW AND BALL

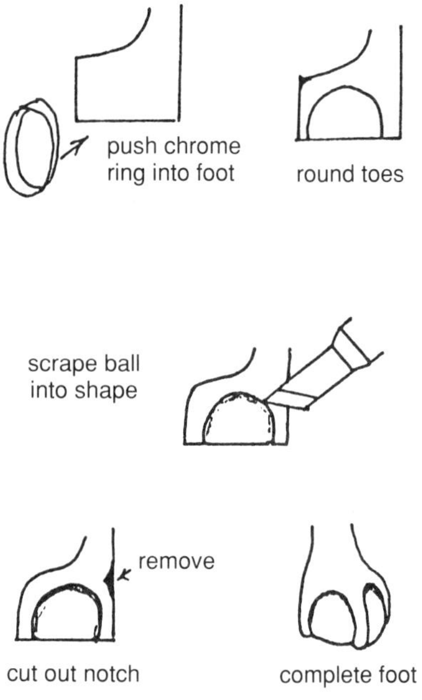

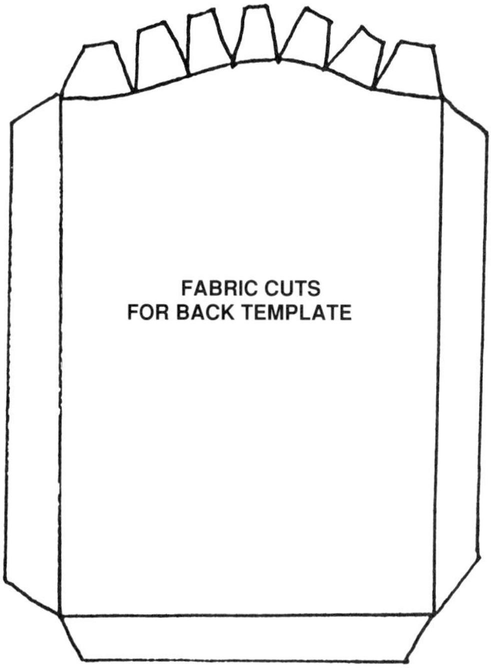

Diagrams

Kit Renderings

CHIPPENDALE LEG

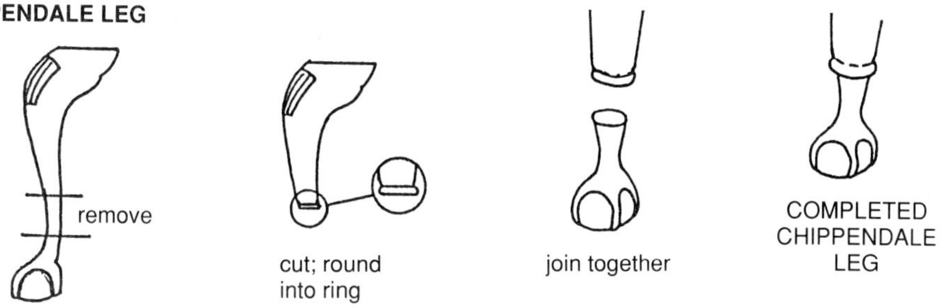

QUEEN ANNE LEG

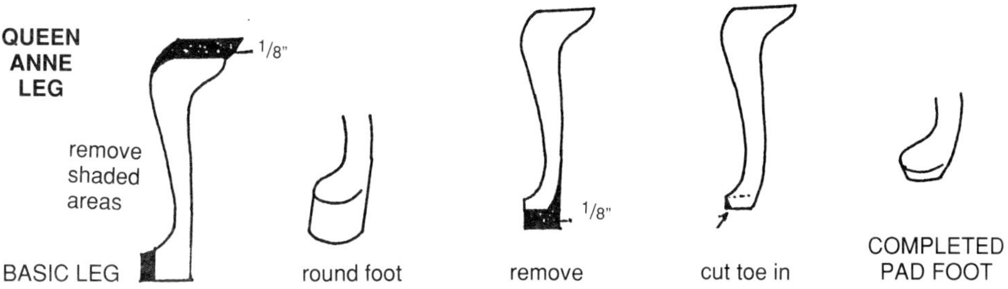

CHIPPENDALE SERPENTINE CHEST c. 1770

A little patience and a few corrections, lovingly applied will yield an "antique" worthy of your mini mansion.

Craftmark's No. 40050 Chippendale Serpentine Chest is one of the most versatile kits available to the collector. The basic kit can be made into any number of different period designs, including the original Chippendale version in this article, a Victorian chest, and a Hepplewhite bowfront chest. Surprisingly, the most complicated modification is in correcting the kit's minor flaws and turning it into a correct Chippendale chest!

Begin by laying out all the parts of the kit on the layout sheet. You will immediately see that this kit has a very shallow serpentine which does not resemble a correct 18th century serpentine. Our first correction will be to deepen this line (see drawing). Parts #77, 84, 85, and 86 will be corrected in the same way. My drawing shows the alterations on part #77, the drawer shelf. This is strictly for your ease in following the instructions.

First draw the deepened serpentine on *only one half* of one shelf (#77). Remove the excess wood with either an X-acto knife or sandpaper wrapped around the handle of the knife (with blade removed). Now do a second shelf divider

using the first as a template. When they are the same, flip the top one over and use it as a guide for the other half. You will now have one shelf divider with equal serpentines on both sides. This is your template for all four dividers and for the drawer fronts.

Remember, when you have done all four, set them on top of one another to be sure they are the same. You may want to use your knife handle wrapped in sandpaper to equalize all pieces. Now use a pencil to trace the corrected line on *both* the top and the bottom of each drawer front. Do not sand these on top of the dividers because you may accidentally deepen the serpentine on the dividers. Place all four drawer fronts together and *gently* sand them together. Switch them about as you sand so that the top and bottom drawers are not oversanded in relation to the others. Once you have completed this step, assemble the drawers with the instructions given in the kit.

If you use the HB Brass hinges I have used, you may wish to wait until the chest is finished before you put the pulls on; otherwise, now is the time to put the holes for the pulls. The hardware included in the kit is not common on serpentine chests, but it is not incorrect.

Now assemble the body of the chest without glue. Note that the sides need only a minor modification to match with the new serpentine. Remove a small amount of wood *on the inside fronts,* next to the drawers (see drawing). You may now glue this section together. Also glue two reeded moldings on the leading edge of the sides. Place the assembled section over the base (#88) and cut a new serpentine just outside the line of the body. The base may now be glued to the bottom of the chest.

MATERIALS AND TOOLS:

- 1 Craftmark No. 40050 Chippendale Serpentine Chest kit
- 1 flat blade X-Acto knife
- Several sheets of very fine grade sandpaper
- Sanding block
- Craftmark's mahogany stain kit
- One strip of Housework's smallest reverse cove molding
- One strip of the same, one size larger
- One strip of Housework's smallest bead molding
- 4 pairs #H-38 brasses
- 4 #E8 escutcheons by HB Brass

*This elegant serpentine chest (**opposite**) can be yours with small corrections and additional touches such as reeded side moldings (**above left**) to the basic kit. Creating straight bracket feet (**above right**) adds authenticity.*

A view from above reveals the now-correct serpentine curve of the top and front of the chest.

The top will be somewhat like the base, but slightly larger. Place the base over the top (#73) and cut a new serpentine *front only* just outside the line of the base. With your sandpaper wrapped over the end of your knife, deepen the front of the side very slightly.

Now comes the most difficult part. The smallest reverse cove molding is glued around the top. To get it around the curve you need to break the wood very slightly. Basswood will actually mold quite nicely to the shape, but this will take some practice, so expect to break a few pieces before you get it right. Since this is supposed to be an antique the eye will be unusually forgiving about cracks and breaks. On the base use the reverse cove molding the next size up. This will require slight cutting on the front of the molding (remove a couple of notches). Now break and glue this molding around the base. I will warn you now, this really needs to be held by *you* until it is dry. Rubber bands will slip and the molding will not dry in the correct position.

The feet in the original kit do not even faintly resemble a period ogee (curved) bracket foot, so we will turn them into straight bracket feet as seen in the photographs. Place the feet under the base molding. Note that they are right on the edge, not set back. Since the new serpentine has changed the line of the inside front, cut all three sides on each foot square. Remove all of the ogee (curved) part of the foot. You will then have a straight bracket foot which, were it on a genuine antique, would be veneered. To simulate this effect, cut a small vertical line at the corner of each foot (see drawing). The back feet need to be cut smaller. Remove enough of the back foot to make it in proportion to the front. Cut the ogee off so that the back feet are the same as the front feet.

The back of the chest on an original antique would consist of two unequal boards. Drop down about 3/4" and score a horizontal line across the back. This will look like authentic 18th century construction.

If you have not already stained your chest, you may wish to try the effects seen on my sample. Any serpentine front will be veneered, otherwise unsightly end grain would show. In miniature, an 18th century veneer can be simulated by streaking the mahogany stain on in a slight swirl. Look at the photographs of originals and you will notice that the drawer fronts mirror one another. In other words, each drawer is the invert of the one above it. The effect is very subtle and not at all like the obvious careful matching of Victorian veneers.

When the stain has dried, use the clear finish to seal it. When that coat has dried, check to be sure you have covered all the *outside* wood. The back and underside are not stained mahogany nor sealed. Once you are sure all that should be sealed is finished and dried, cover the piece with "glaze" stain, then wipe it off leaving rather dull highlights in the crevices and on the edges. Note that the insides are never stained and that the back and underside can be stained with the "glaze" stain used full strength and *without* the clear sealer.

The final touch is the HB Brass hardware. The placement is evident from the photographs, but one should note how low the escutcheons (keyhole covers) are. Period locks are very large; therefore the keyholes are located well down from the top of each drawer.

Were this chest a full size antique, very few of us would be able to afford it, but with a bit of patience and not an awful lot of work, we can create our own Chippendale Serpentine Chest, c. 1770 that would be the envy of the finest museum.

DIAGRAMS FOR CHIPPENDALE SERPENTINE CHEST

SHELF DIVIDERS

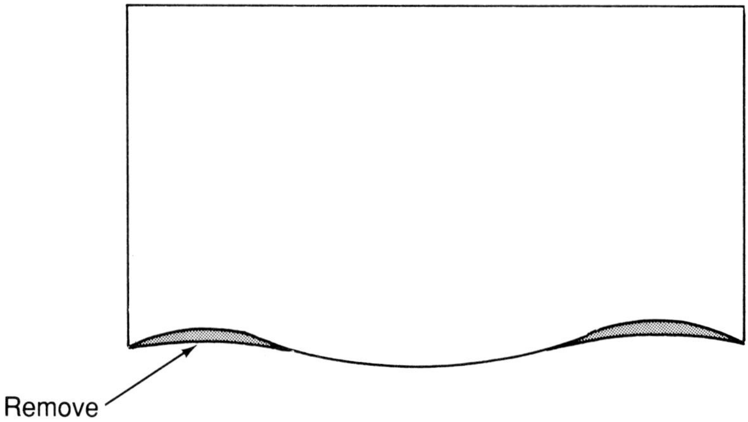

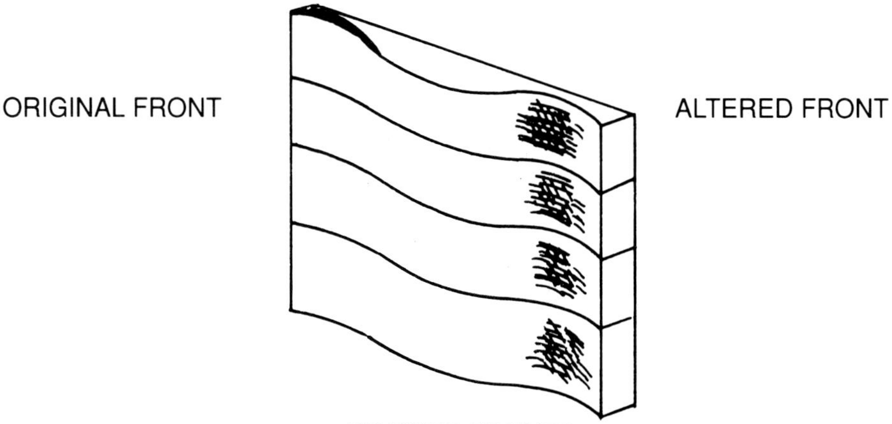

DRAWER FRONTS

DIAGRAMS FOR CHIPPENDALE SERPENTINE CHEST

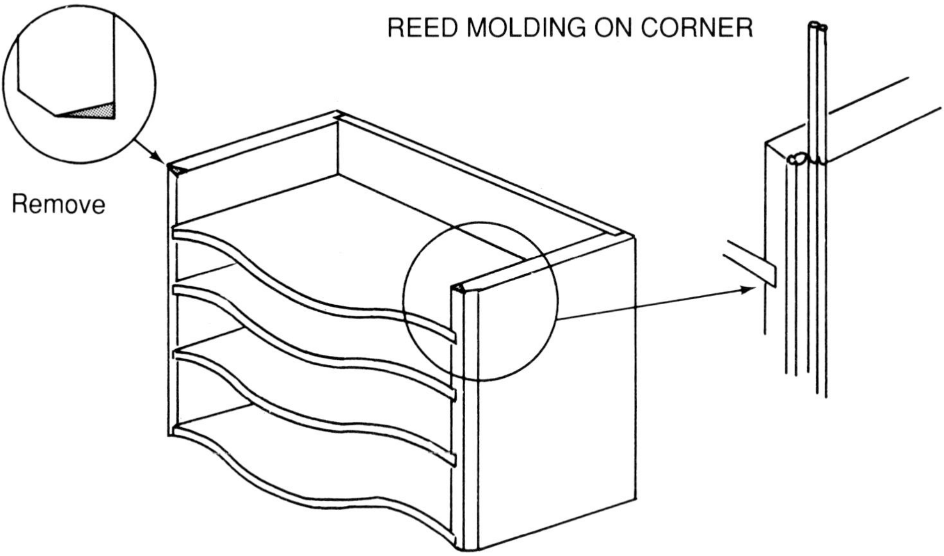

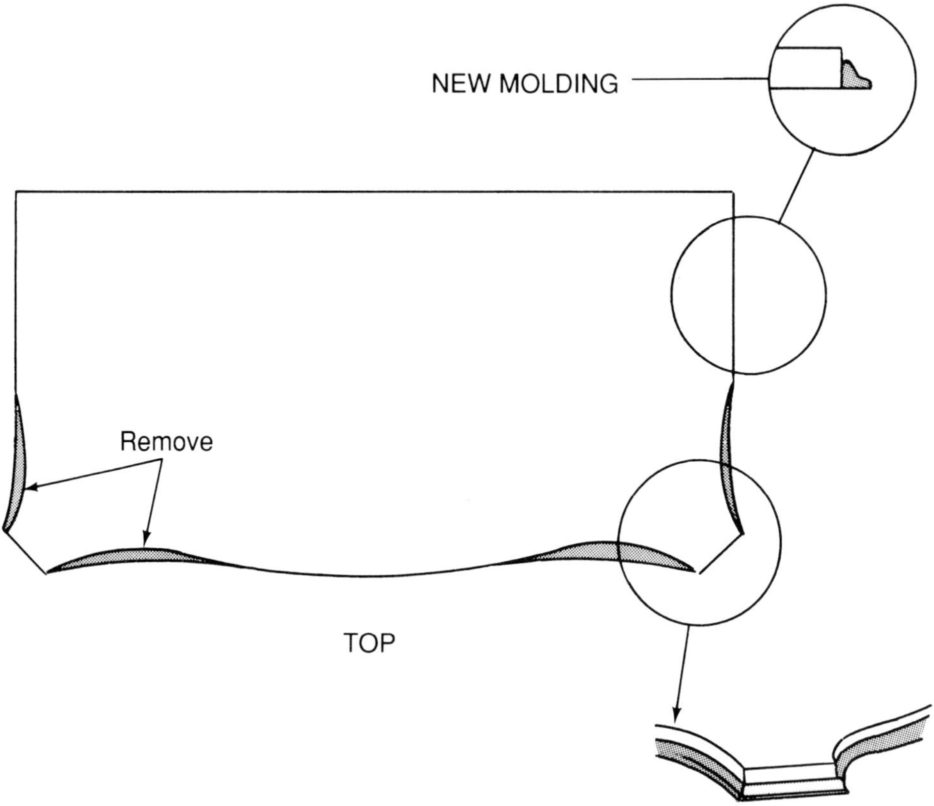

DIAGRAMS FOR CHIPPENDALE SERPENTINE CHEST

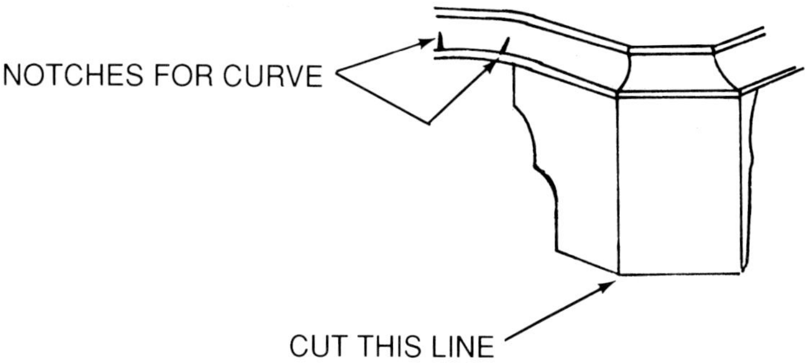

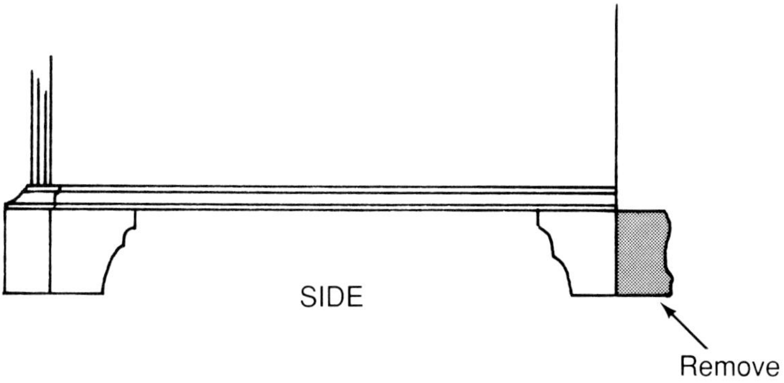

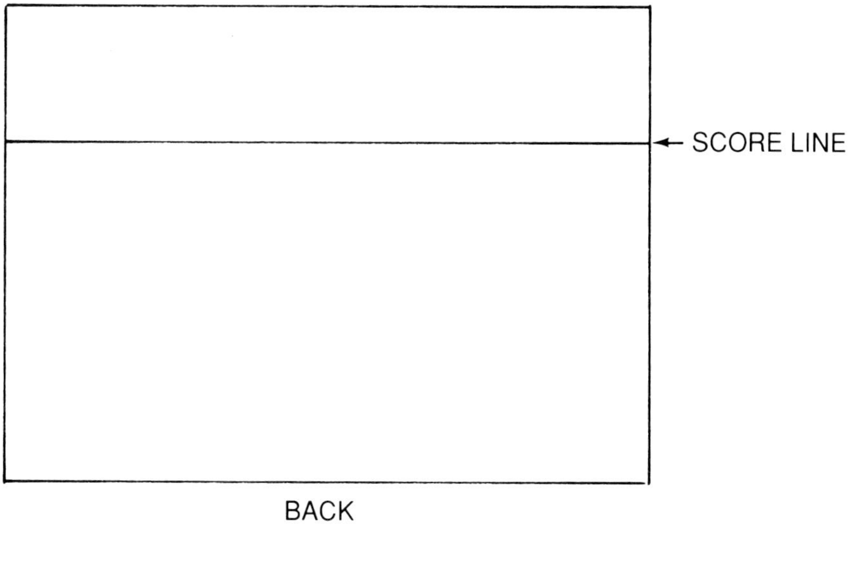

Formal Upholstery

A shell detail here, a bit of fabric there — and voila! you've created a keepsake!

HOUSE OF MINIATURES #40027 Cabriole Leg Chippendale Arm Chair offers the craftsman a number of interesting variations. I have chosen to make an upholstered back arm chair. This is a more formal and important piece than the side chairs in the kit.

INSTRUCTIONS

Begin with the seat. Using the instructions in steps 1 and 2, assemble the seat. Install part #7 upside down so that the sculpted side is facing up. Omit part #13. Glue an additional board the same thickness to each side (see drawing). Notch hole for arms next to the same location as original hole.

When seat is complete, round all top edges toward the outside (see drawing). This will soften the edge of the seat when it is upholstered. Next, add cardboard and foam seat which is provided for slip seat. Unlike the kit instructions, we will glue this into place. Then cut a thin piece of foam plastic to the shape of top with a little extra in front to cover gap on part #7. Make cutouts for the arms just over notches on the sides. Glue this foam on top of the entire seat.

The best type of foam to use is packing foam for shipping full-sized furniture. This is free for the asking at most furniture shops. They will have several types of foam — just pick the one you like best. Take a pair of sharp scissors or you may end up taking more than you want.

When the seat is complete, upholster it with fabric. If you cut the corners fairly close you can get a nice sharp edge on the corners. Use an X-Acto knife to make a small slit in the fabric where notches for the arms will be. Set this part aside until later.

Our back is almost entirely new. I used the legs and uprights, parts #3 and 4, and glued a piece of matboard between them. Use my template for the correct size and lines. I cut small pieces of basswood to fill in the rest of the uprights since our back is 1/4" taller than the original uprights (see drawing). If I were to do this kit again, I would cut the legs off 1-1/2" from the floor and increase both the rake of the legs and the rake of the back (see drawing). This would look more authentic and high-style, but is not necessary if your chair is to be viewed from the front only. Sand a bit off back legs. The kit legs are slightly wider at the bottom. This is not authentic.

Use foam to upholster the back. You need to cut foam at an angle near the top. This will give you a rounded look appropriate for the chair. Cut foam short so that it stops at the seat line. This is now ready to upholster. Note in the photograph that if you are using a stripe you need to match the stripe where the seat and back join.

Use a small piece of manila folder covered in fabric to finish off back (see drawing). This is the last piece to be put on the chair. Do not install it now.

I have shown suggested cuttings to aid in upholstering. I used Velverette glue to upholster my chair. If you are careful it is possible to glue upholstery directly to parts that show. Test your fabric first. Some fabrics will always have to be glued at out-of-sight locations. Set this entire piece aside until later. *Do not glue now.* By the way, if this is to be a period chair, do not overstuff. Period backs were very thin by today's standards.

Now we will alter the front legs. Cut two small vertical slits on each leg to simulate the wings which are separate pieces on period chairs (see drawing and photograph). This shell knee is the simplest and best one I have done. I used the chrome ring from a ballpoint pen for the entire shell. Lightly sketch shell onto the knees. Push chrome ring into your drawn lines. In my drawing note especially how I get the side detail on the shell. The lovely "carved" detail is done with a penny! I sketched where I wanted indentation, then pushed the penny into those lines. Since this detail will get a light sanding and antiquing, the pencil lines will not show.

The claw and ball foot is also created with a chrome ring bent into an oval and pushed into all four sides of each foot. I deepened the ball by scraping an X-Acto knife along this detail (see drawing). Both of these legs were remarkably hard, so one authentic detail has been omitted. I wanted to use a tool for removing press-type to "sculpt" the toe detail just above the ball. I have done this before with good results. This is shown in my drawings. Not all of these kits have such firm wood (the companion chair in my kit had softer wood). You also need to notch the back of the leg to give an authentic line to the foot (see drawing).

*Ron shows us how to create a more formal upholstered arm chair (**opposite**) from House of Miniatures' Cabriole Leg Chippendale arm chair kit.*

*This view (**above**) shows how important it is to match up stripes on the seat and the back for a finished look. Notice also the shell detail on the knees and the ball and claw feet.*

Slightly round the tops of your cabriole so that the legs appear to fit the seat (see drawing). The seat is not at a right angle, but the legs are. I forgot to do this and, as the photograph shows, the front legs appear to stick out slightly. This is a reason not to pre-finish parts.

The arms require considerable more modification. My measurements will be approximate since most of us will glue the back at a slightly different angle. I cut 1/4" from each arm. If you make the sharper rake I suggested earlier, you will remove less. Use two straight pins to hold back in place where you intend to glue it. This allows you to adjust arm length as necessary.

Instead of parts #50 for arm supports, I used part #8, the yoke, cut in half with some wood removed (see drawing). This is not an authentic line, but it is much closer than the support provided in the kit. I have a correct support in the drawings should you wish to make it from scratch. I changed this because we need a higher arm and a straighter support. Round

In this photo, you can see that the support and arm join are slightly rounded. Ron used part #8, the yoke (cut in half) for the support, rather than the ones provided in the kit.

both front and back where shown.

The actual arm will make a very fragile connection with the new support. Reinforce the connection with a drop of glue inside the join. The glue can be hidden with the antiquer; but first reshape the top and bottom of each arm. Follow the instructions in my drawings and look carefully at the photographs. You will see the support and the arm join are slightly rounded. Small details like these add much to your piece.

Glue arms to the back of the chair. Notice you may glue these near the front or right at the back. Either detail will look authentic. Your supports will glue into the slit you made in the fabric. It is surprising how neatly this glues into the slit without any special measuring. One caution: the slender connection of the arm and support will always be slightly fragile. Remember to put a drop of glue behind the join (see drawing).

If you have not prefinished the pieces, do so now. The back legs must be prefinished since they are to be upholstered over the finish. All wood that shows should be stained with Craftmark's mahogany stain. If you want a walnut finish, use 3/4's of Craftmark's mahogany stain mixed with 1/4 of Craftmark's walnut stain. Their walnut stain is much too dark as it comes. Whichever you choose, finish it with their clear finish, then wipe a small amount of "glaze" stain over the details to highlight them. This will hide the flaws and accentuate the carved details.

Two modifications you may prefer: if you want to match the serpentine of the back with a serpentine on the seat rail, use a thin piece of cardboard just slightly longer than the seat front. Glue at each end. This will buckle out slightly and form a serpentine front. You can slip a small wedge of wood or put a bit of glue behind the curve to support it. Remember this is a very slight curve. Don't overdo it (see drawing).

The other modification is to have a straight top instead of the serpentine. Simply substitute the straight template for the serpentine when you get to that part. You still need to cut your foam at an angle to get a smooth top line.

I based this chair on some New York chairs, c. 1770. At current prices they would sell in excess of $50,000 each. At those prices our Craftmark kit is a steal as well as a treasure!

Diagrams

Kit Renderings

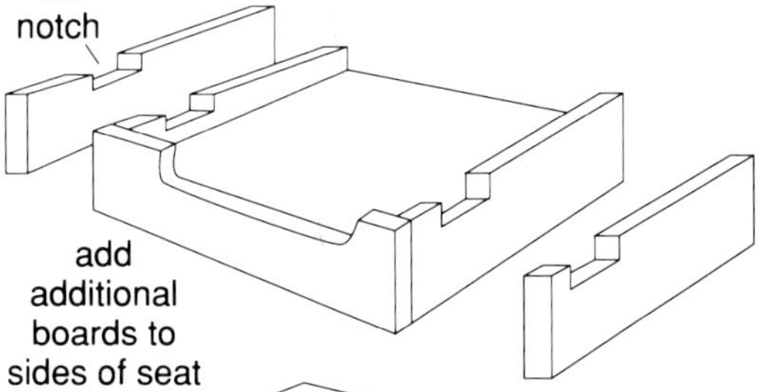

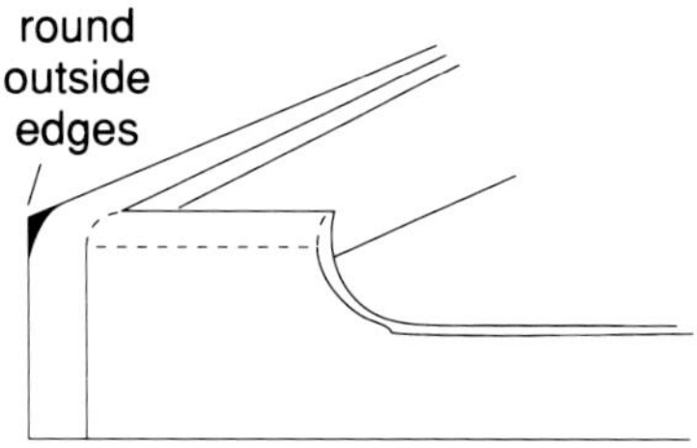

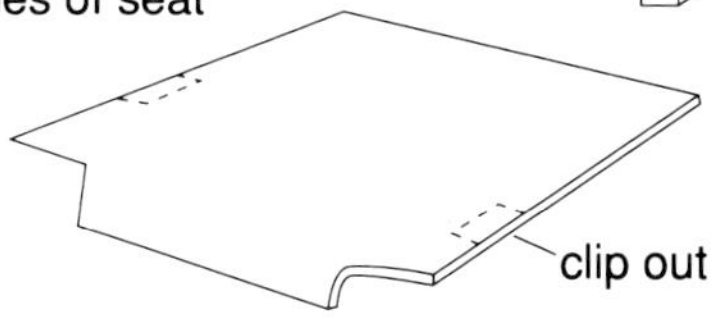

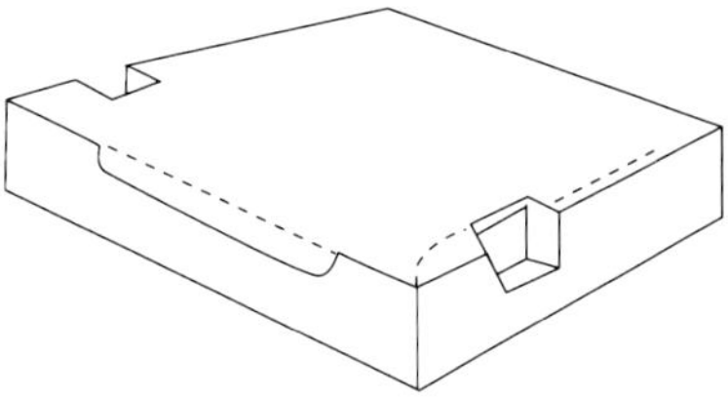

seat with foam in place - notches cut out for arms

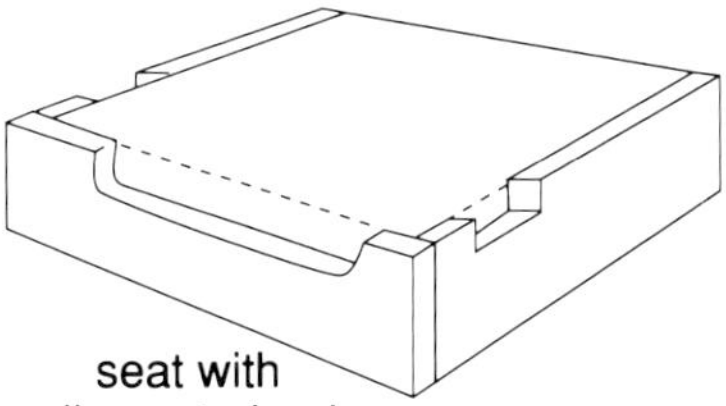

seat with slip seat glued in place - new foam ready to glue

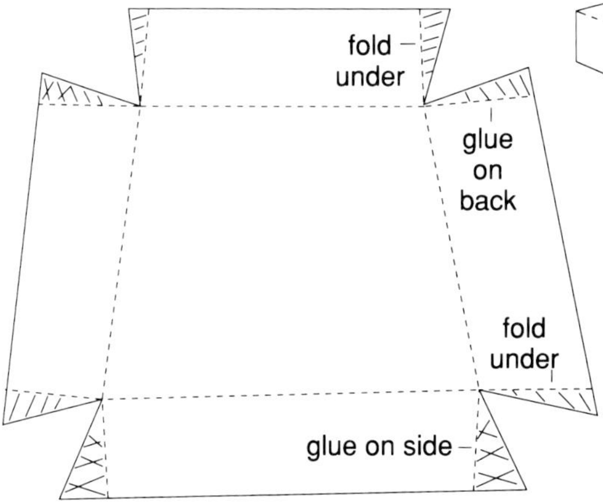

top view fabric cutting detail

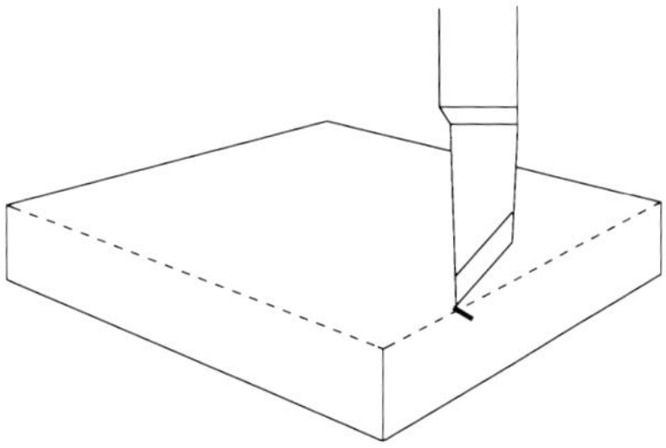

cut fabric at notch

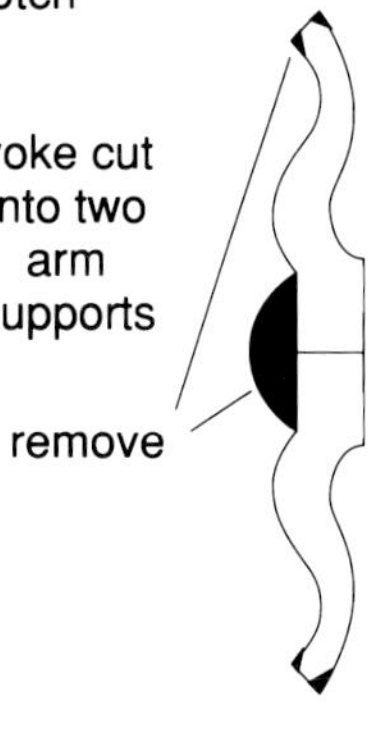

yoke cut into two arm supports

Diagrams

Kit Renderings

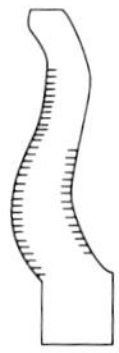

round edges

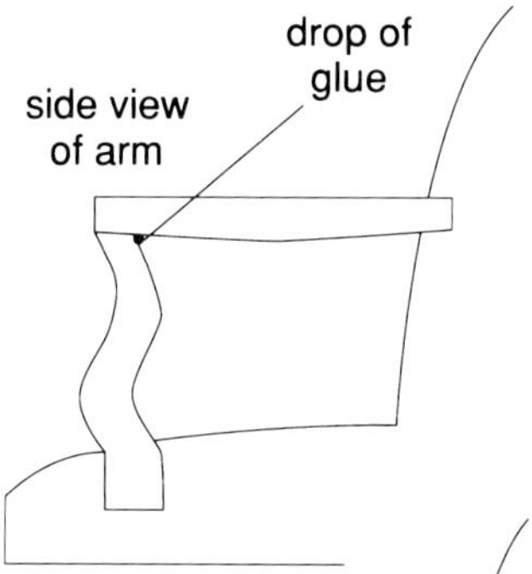

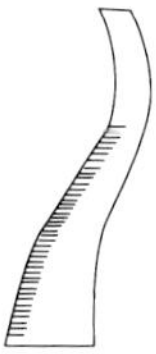

correct arm design

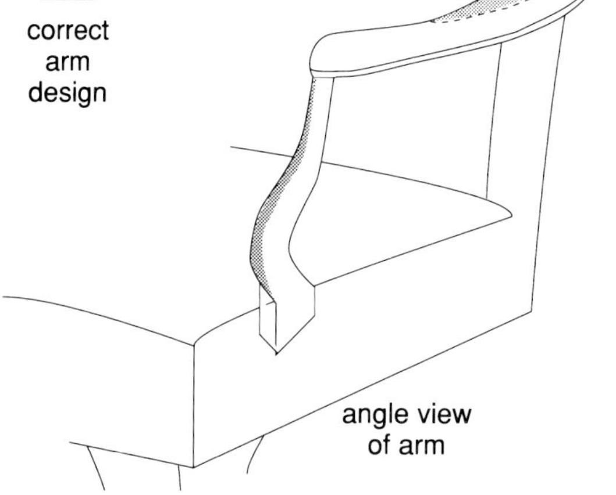

angle view of arm

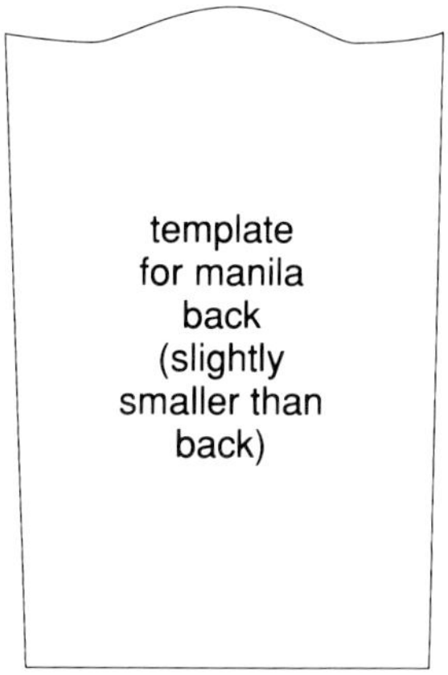

Diagrams

Kit Renderings

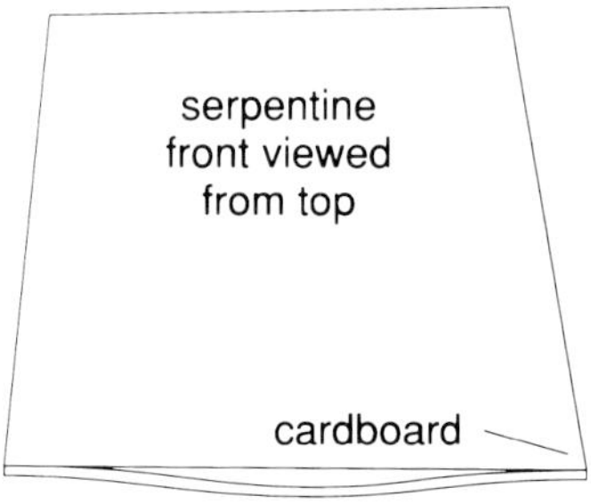

seat
line
cut
here
do not
cut dotted
line

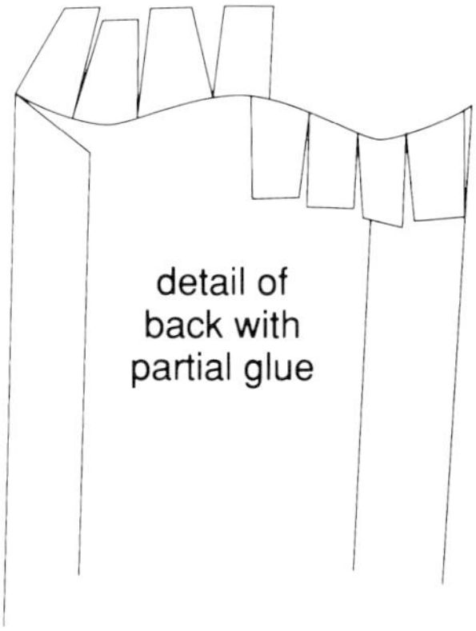

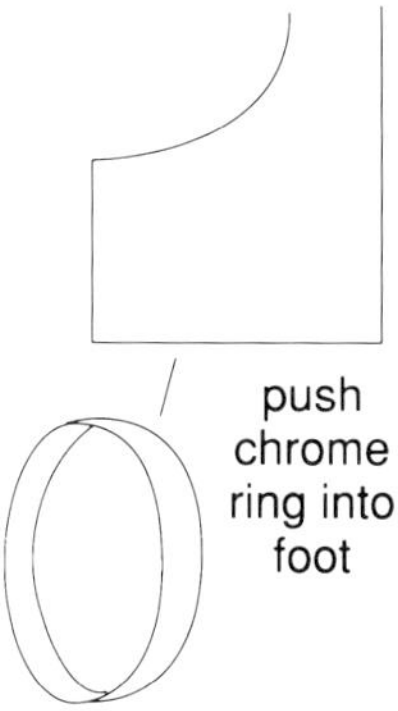

push
chrome
ring into
foot

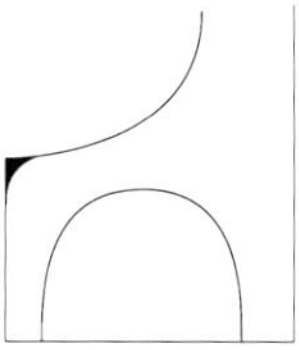

round toes

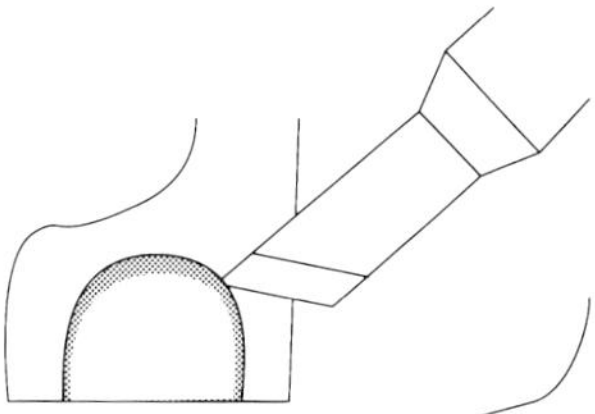

scrape
ball into
shape

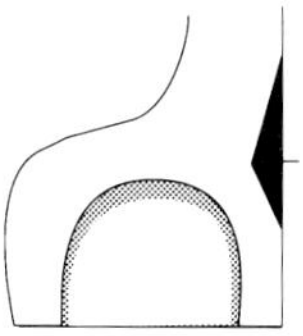

remove

cut notch
out

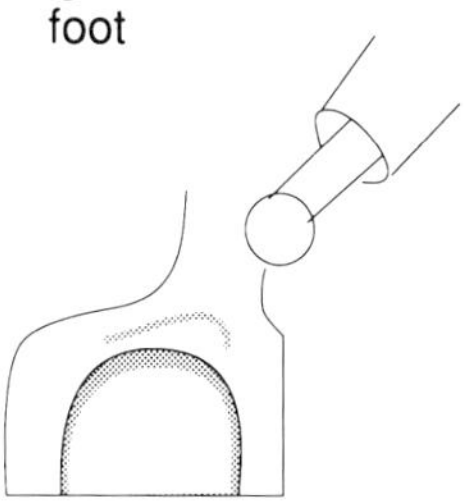

shape with
press-type tool

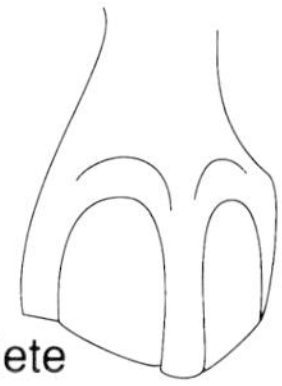

complete
foot

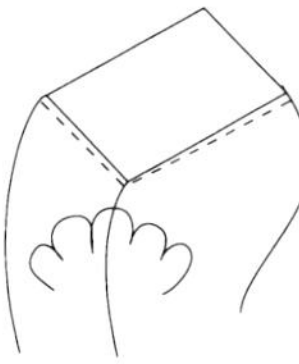

sand to
round

top of leg

Diagrams

Kit Renderings

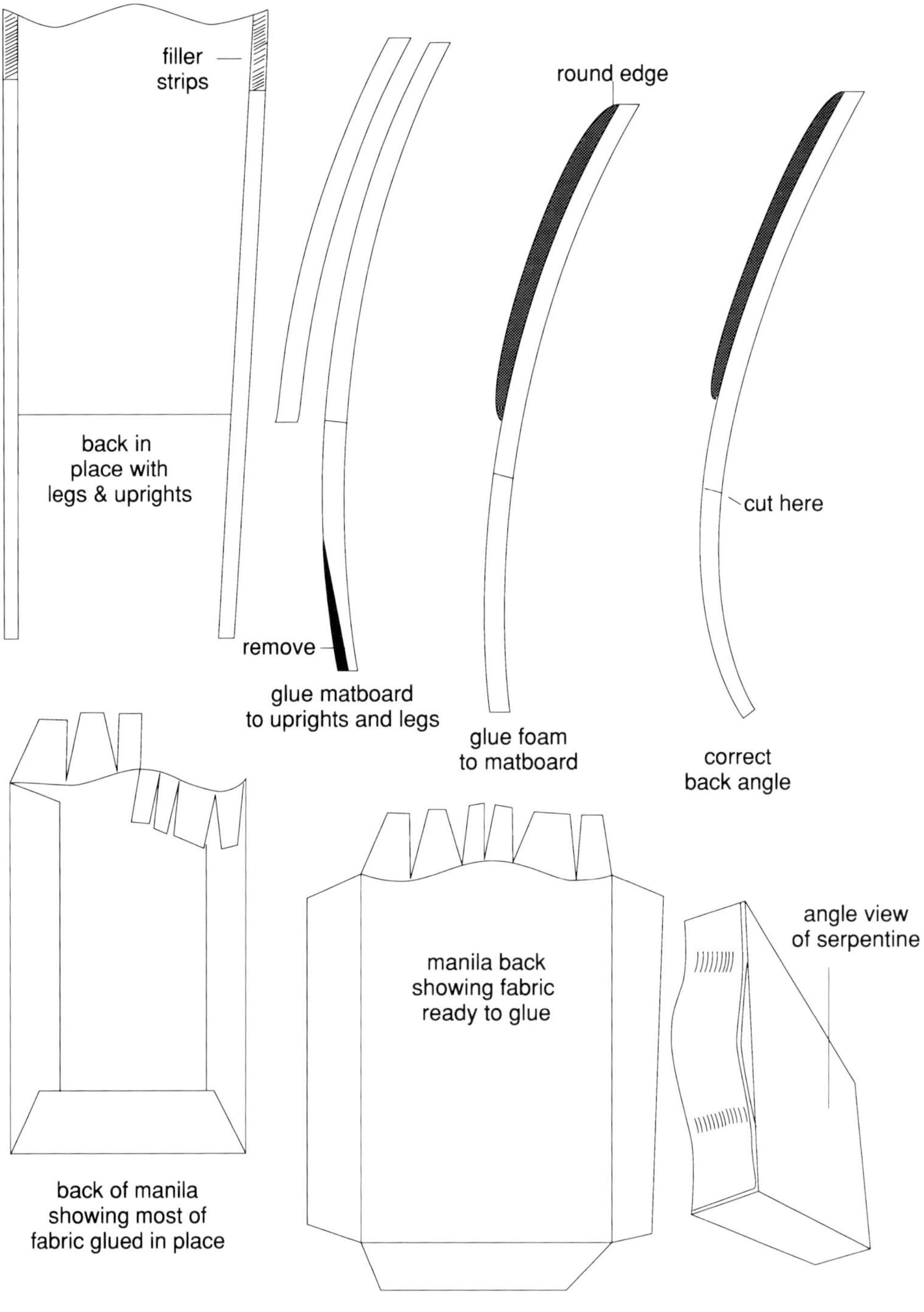

Diagrams

Kit Renderings

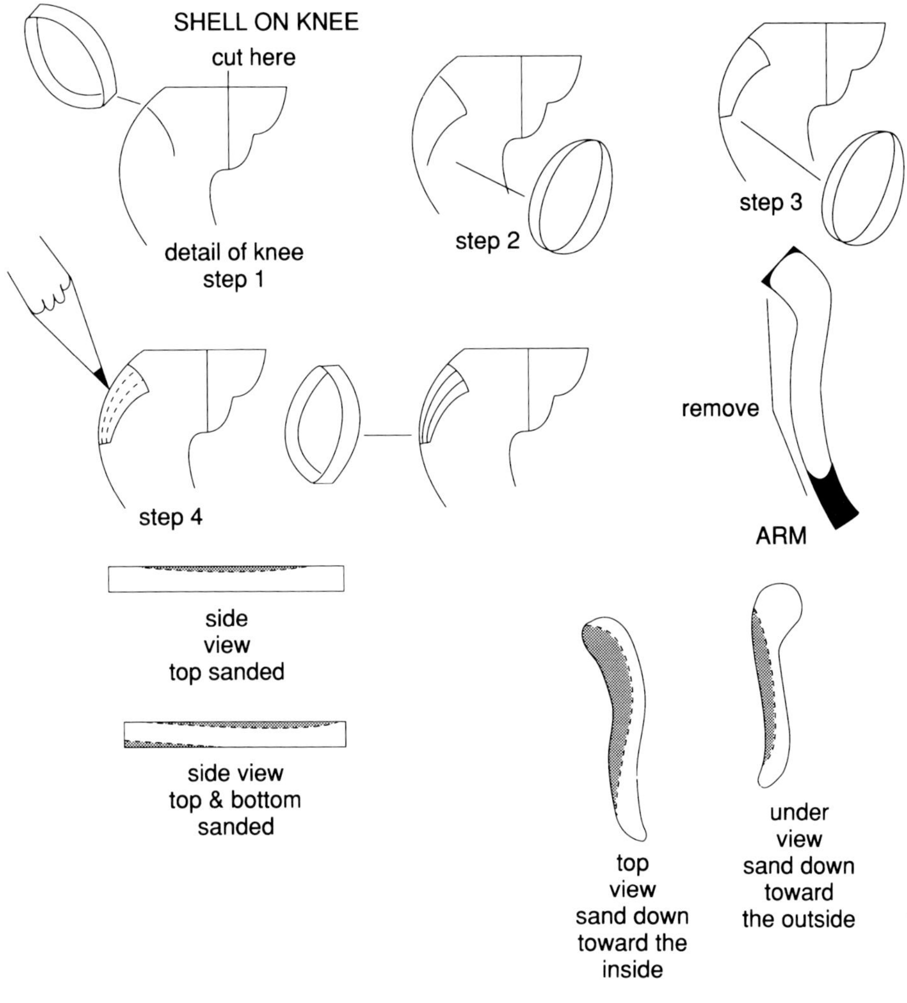

CHIPPENDALE HANGING SHELF

With a little cosmetic surgery, this kit adds a graceful note to any setting

When most of us think of miniatures we think "thin and delicate." One exception to this might be the many furniture kits available. Most are over-built, perhaps with the philosophy that the average collector is more klutz than craftsman. Whatever the reason, our alterations to the hanging shelf will lighten the kit and make it more authentic.

The thick divider, part #91 on the instruction sheet will be the first part we alter. Remove all of the upper sections of this divider. No 18th century craftsman would be so insecure in his art as to use such a heavy and awkward divider. Don't discard the upper part, we will use it later.

The fretwork sides need to be trimmed of the "flash," those superfluous pieces of wood sticking out at the top and bottom. Remove these with your hobby knife, taking care not to break these fragile parts. You may find it helpful to put a piece of masking tape on any piece you are going to cut. This will help strengthen the wood. Naturally you remove the tape after you've finished cutting. Use your fine grade sandpaper to finish the rough edges. Don't worry about rounding the edges. Most 18th century shelves such as this have rounded edges (see drawing), but note that the lower part should remain squared. The fretwork itself will need little sanding. You may use a small file or tightly rolled sandpaper. Do not over sand. The fretwork needs only the removal of rough edges to look fine.

MATERIALS

- 1 Craftmark #40032 Chippendale hanging shelf,
- 1 flat blade hobby knife, small file, fine grade sandpaper
- Craftmark's mahogany finishing kit
- HB Brass #H 9 pulls.

Now we will work on the shelves themselves. Since we will not be using the center support, the shelves will have gaps in the center. I suggest cutting new shelves using the ones from the kit as a guide for size, but you may prefer to use only what is found in the kit. You may plug the gaps by gluing in strips of wood taken from the discarded top of part #91. If you do this the shelves will be installed with the gap at the

*Re-crafting the Chippendale hanging shelf (**above**) from a standard kit ywill yield a more authentic accessory.*

back rather than the way shown on the instruction sheet. All of the shelves will need this treatment except the bottom section with the drawer. If you choose to retain these shelves, when it's finished you will want to cover the plugs with something decorative — perhaps a book or a statue

The drawers are assembled as shown in the instructions. You may wish to buy different brasses. The pulls in the kit are correct, but bail pulls (see drawing) are more common. Bail brasses will also need a plain escutcheon (a keyhole cover) above the pull (see drawing). The drawers are a bit too large to work properly. Sand down the outside edges and the drawer bottom and sides. Use a block of wood behind your sandpaper to insure that the drawer edges remain square. Sand *all* sides, otherwise your beveled edge will be off center.

An alternate version of the shelf is made by eliminating the entire center piece (#91) and one drawer and cutting the width by half. Instead of a wide shelf with two drawers, you will have a narrow shelf with a single drawer. This version is especially nice as part of a pair of shelves on either side of a mantle, but of course you will need another kit. Should you make the narrow version, reverse the drawer front so that the bevel is not showing. Narrow shelves need simple drawer fronts to complement the complexity of the fret. This version also looks best with bail brasses.

I suggest staining the shelf before you assemble it. A very light coat of Craftmark's mahogany stain will give the best effect. Should you be doing a Victorian room in which the shelf would be a 19th century reproduction, a walnut stain is also fine, but mix in a tad of mahogany stain to counter the blandness of the standard walnut stain. When the entire kit is assembled, use the clear finish sealer over the mahogany. If this is a period room the shelf would be new, so you are finished. If your shelf is an "antique," brush on the "glaze" stain in the corners and spread the dark shadow out from there. Even after the glaze is dry you have a great deal of flexibility. You can add and remove the glaze until you get the exact look you want. Do not follow the instructions in the stain kit; the results will not look genuine.

And there you have it — one of the most valuable small antiques of the 18th century is yours to fill with tiny treasures.

DIAGRAMS FOR CHIPPENDALE HANGING SHELF

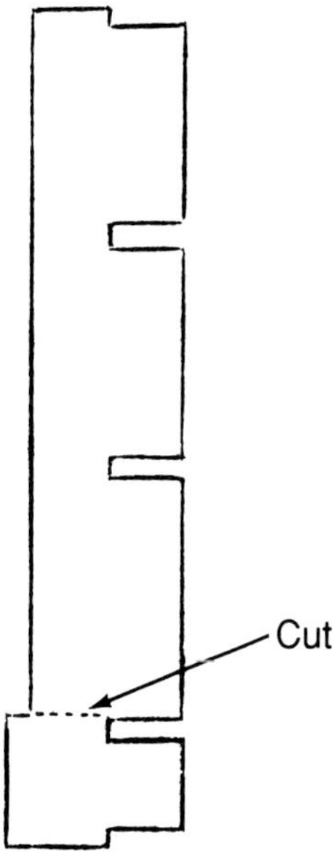

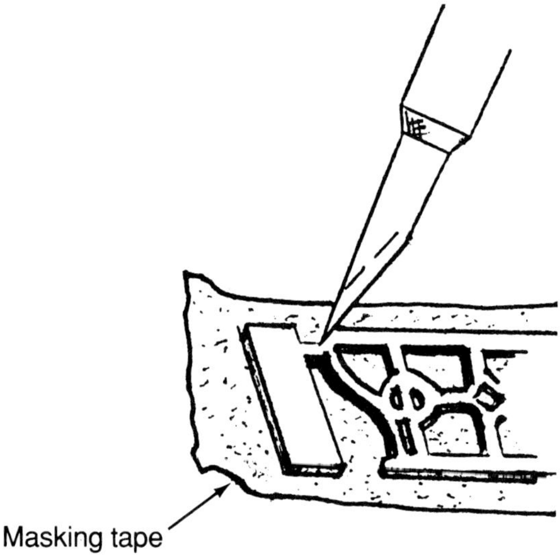

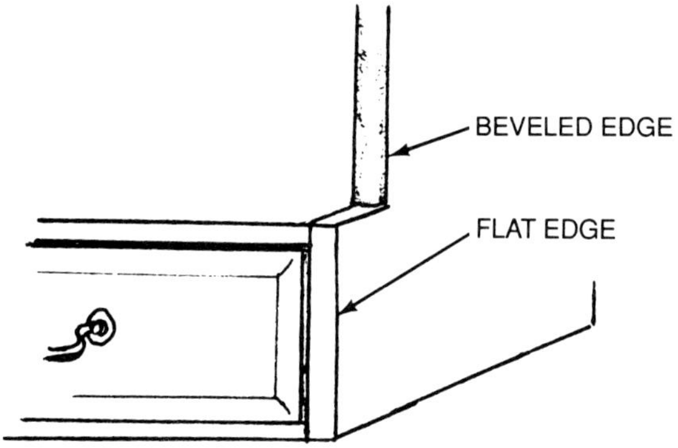

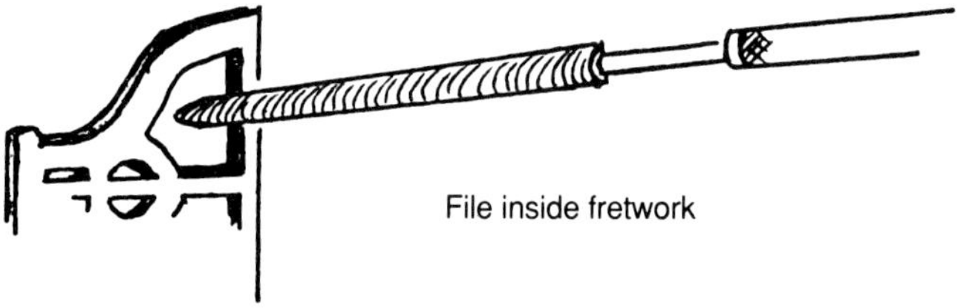

DIAGRAMS FOR CHIPPENDALE HANGING SHELF

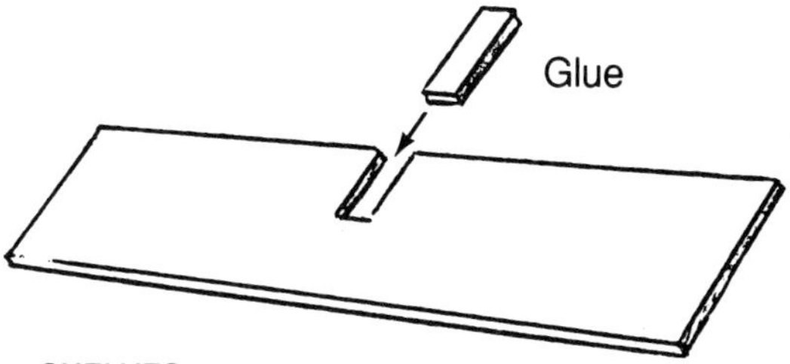

SHELVES

ESCUTCHEON

DRAWER FRONT w/ BAIL BRASSES

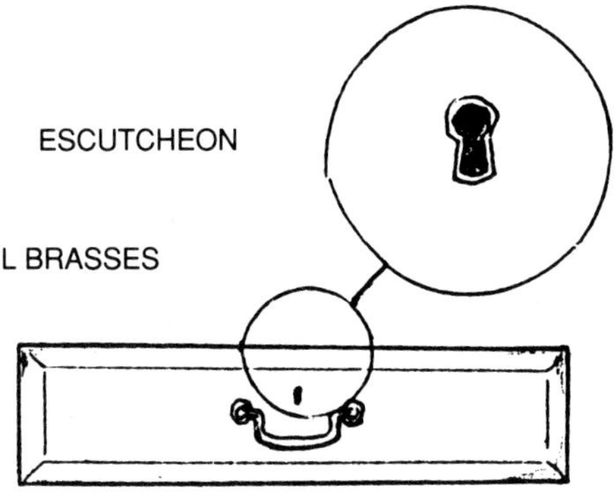

SHELF w/ SINGLE DRAWER

Beauty and the Breakfront

Transform a simple Chippendale into a princess of a Hepplewhite

CRAFTMARK'S CHIPPENDALE BREAKFRONT, #40048, presents the perfect opportunity for the craftsman to display fine accessories in a lovely manner. Our breakfront is changed into a Hepplewhite breakfront c. 1780. This allows us to use somewhat simpler lines and "inlay" detail. Instead of four doors on the lower section, we have two in the center and two banks of drawers on either side. If you prefer, you may omit the drawers and retain all four doors.

INSTRUCTIONS

Begin by assembling the cornice board (parts 66 and 67) and the base (parts 43 and 44) following instructions in the kit. Score the top of the cornice as shown in my drawing. Genuine breakfronts were in six parts, not two. We can get this effect by scoring the top. You may wish to complete the effect on the back (see drawing); but since this piece will undoubtedly be displayed against a wall, most of you will only score the front.

I used a small piece of 1/8" cove molding to continue the cornice. I wanted to use dentil molding, but I was told that simple dentil mold-

MATERIALS

- One Craftmark #40048 Chippendale Breakfront
- 1/8" Midwest cover molding
- Strip of dentil molding (optional)
- Scrap of basswood approx. 1/2" x 1/16" x 1/2"
- 1/4" dowel
- Realife's #857 Colonial bedposts (optional)
- Paper doily
- House of Miniatures Mahogany finishing kit
- Minicolor's Jamestown Colony red
- Accent Country Colors #2431 Wild Honey
- 1/4" square strip of basswood
- Wood glue
- Evergreen Scale Models .015 sheet styrene
- Two strips Midwest 1/16" double bead molding
- Two strips Midwest 1/16" square molding
- 1/4" x 1/8" strip of basswood
- Toothpick
- Midwest baseboard molding with shoe
- Green water-base paint
- Several small scraps of basswood
- Gold foil
- Two sets #S-10 Hepplewhite pulls by Suzanne Russo
- One set #S-20 Hepplewhite oval escutcheon by Suzanne Russo
- Scraps of colored paper from magazines

*Create this Hepplewhite breakfront (**opposite**) from Craftmark's Chippendale breakfront kit and Ron Benson's ingenious techniques. Ron used part of a doily for the "carved" decoration at the top of the broken arch (**above**).*

ing unattached to cornice molding had been discontinued. I've included this option in the drawings since some of you may have dentil molding or may be willing to cut it off a cornice molding.

Next we will improve the broken arch, parts 68, 69, and 70. I did not use the finial. These three parts are twice as thick as they should be. Cut the depth of each down by at least 1/8". Using the drawings as templates, reshape the broken arches and centerpiece to show a continual curve. The center, part 68, will have to be flattened to accept the new pediment, which is flat without a finial. You may use this pediment to display porcelain, attach a finial, or leave it empty. The finial from Realife's #857 Colonial bedposts would be perfect.

Our new pediment is cut from basswood 1/4" deep x 1/16" thick. It is just under 1/2" wide, but if you cut a deeper curve into part 68 it will need to be narrower. With very fine sandpaper sand the insides (open pores) of parts 69 and 70. When it is smooth, apply a thin coat of Craftmark's clear sealer to this area. Be very careful not to get the sealer on any other part of the wood. This seals the pores and will allow you to have a uniform color when you stain these parts.

The rounded ends of the broken arch are 1/4" dowels cut and glued to the ends. The lovely "carved" rosettes are carefully cut from a paper doily painted "mahogany" with Minicolor's Jamestown Colony red and glued to the ends of the dowels. Note that the rosettes match vertically (see photograph). To strengthen the rosettes, use a toothpick to apply wood glue to the back. Use it to fill in the recessed area. Let it dry and then apply a bit more until it feels strong. Paint over the dry glue with the same paint. One hint — doilies are usually stamped unevenly. Before you cut out your rosette, look for deep, well-stamped detail. Glue this entire assembly to the top of part 67.

Assemble the top half following the instruction in steps 4, 5, and 6. I eliminated a couple of shelves to allow a larger space for two urns. Period breakfronts would have had even more slots to allow shelf adjustment. If you want to add more grooves so that your shelves are in different locations, that is authentic.

Our "glass" doors are considerably altered from the originals. The printed clear panels provided in the kit are incorrect period design. There is no way to use them if you want authenticity. Instead I cut new clear panels from .015 sheet styrene. Do not cut these until you have assembled the doors. We need a strip of 1/4" x 1/8" basswood to replace parts 49 on the two inside doors. Assemble the two outside doors at this time. When they are dry, use them as a template to cut new "glass" (see drawing). Set these aside until later.

*Suzanne Russo's escutcheons and drawer pulls add a beautiful touch to the breakfront (**above**), as does the green "inlay" on the doors.*

The two center doors are widened fractionally, well under 1/32". This is done because we are not using part #50, which covered the gap between the doors. The new fractionally wider doors will almost meet. Install the brass pins and try these in place. When they are correct, cut new windows as you did previously.

The molding on the doors is a simple 18th century design. It is also correct to have only two panels of glass per door. See drawings for both designs. I opted for simple doors since most collectors will want to show off small collectables on the shelves. More complicated designs make it more difficult to see the shelves.

I used the smallest double bead molding (1/16") by Midwest for all door fronts. Before you assemble any of this, sand the molding and stain and finish it. If you don't do this first you will get either stain or finish on your "glass." I also used Midwest 1/16" square molding for the inside molding. This I painted Jamestown Colony red before I cut it. This will have no other finish.

Use my drawing to cut and miter the wood. The double bead molding fits flush inside the doors. Follow the measurements on my drawing. Expect some difficulty in getting the cross molding to fit at a correct right angle. You can adjust the cross molding by cutting a little off the top or bottom of one side (see drawing). Do not glue at this time.

The tiny square molding fits on the back. I wanted a tight functional fit, so I did not miter this molding. Instead I cut the two short ends, then cut the longer pieces (see drawing). This should be a very tight fit. Cut two cross moldings for each door. Here's the secret. If you install the back first, without glue, and then install the front, you can sandwich the "glass" between and see exactly what your doors look like before you glue. If there are any corrections, they can be made now.

When you are satisfied, remove the bead molding. With a toothpick apply glue on the door edge and re-install the moldings. Glue the tops and bottoms first, then the sides, then the cross moldings. The latter are glued with a single drop of glue on each end (see drawing). Turn the door over and remove the square molding. Apply glue in the same manner along the door edges. Again install the tops and bottoms first, then the sides, and finally the cross moldings. Be sure to get these exactly behind the front moldings. This is what makes the door look as if it has three pieces of glass instead of one. Repeat for the other doors.

Our lower half has a good many alterations. Starting with the top, part 57, I applied a 1/4" molded edge to the entire lip. This molding is not exactly correct. You may apply the very smallest half-round molding available in the center for an even richer look (see drawing). Assemble the lower case as shown in step 3 of the instructions. Glue this on the base, parts 43 and 44.

The doors go together as shown on your instructions sheet; however, we will use them backwards. Therefore we need to make our "inlay" and "veneer" before gluing these together. I made an "inlay" mistake on my doors which is corrected on the drawings. Score the lines where I have indicated. *Note*: I have also scored a number of "cracks" in the cross-banding. This will add authencity. We will discuss finishing techniques here because these doors should be finished before installation.

I have painted a green "inlay" around each door. This simulates hardwood, a generic term for any wood stained green, and a very popular alteration throughout the 18th century. The beautiful matched "crotch mahogany" is Jamestown Colony red greatly thinned and swirled on in matched patterns. Our "carved" patera is from another doily painted Jamestown Colony red and finished. All of this is given a light mahogany stain afterward. You need a bit of filler wood behind the two lower doors and between them. Glue this to the fronts of parts 52 and between the doors.

My drawers are only fronts, but in my drawings there are instructions to make complete drawers. Use the drawings to get the correct sizes of the drawers and openings.

I have given each drawer an "inlay" of crossbanding. This is easy to do. Use a wooden steel-edge ruler. Trace around each drawer with an X-Acto knife. Miter the corners. I painted on a fine vertical crossbanding, but it is just as easy to use your knife to cut a number of fine lines into the cross-banding. This will show up when you put on your final finish.

Since we have eliminated the end doors, we need to bring the drawers out a bit. You need four new pieces of wood the size of parts 45, except fractionally longer. These are to be glued to each side of our drawer slides. The slides will glue between these new pieces. You need six slides. Place them where I have indicated on my drawings.

If you use only the drawer fronts, simply glue a small block of wood to the back of each drawer front and then glue the fronts to the slides. Do not install until you have attached the pulls.

The base, parts 43 and 44, is much too short and squat for an 18th century design. I added a new deeper molding to my base. This is Midwest's baseboard molding which had a small shoe molding attached. Remove the shoe molding (see drawing) and miter and glue behind the molding. You will need to cut new feet to glue behind the molding. I used 1/4" square basswood. Should you plan to have your piece seen from the back you will need four extra feet at the center (see drawing).

In the photographs you can see "locks" on the doors. These are small pieces of gold foil paper cut to size and glued on. The left hand center door has only a small rectangle of gold, since it would not have a complete lock. Our wonderful oval pulls and escutcheons are by Suzanne Russo. If you want a more Chippendale feel, use her bail brasses, #S-22.

Our finish is Craftmark's Mahogany finish. As usual I stained the piece, used the clear finish and antiqued it with the "glaze" finish over the top. This latter finish can be adjusted to be as dark or light as you like. Note on the photograph how this highlights the "carving."

I painted the inside "Wild Honey." You may also stain it mahogany, paint it ivory, or Jamestown Colony red, which I used on the inside backs of the doors and all the unseen parts. This is much like genuine "Sheraton red" seen on late 18th century furniture. I used the "glaze" stain on the top since tops tend to get very dirty and black.

*You can create books like these (**above**) to fill your breakfront.*

Our books are small bits of wood covered with shiny paper from magazines or catalogs. To make them look authentic, make several sets in the same color. Try not to get them exactly alike. Genuine books in sets are often discolored and stained. Cut your paper slightly larger than the "pages," fold the top over a bit, then fold the bottom so that the edge of the book is just above the "pages." Glue them on, then cut the ends with scissors (see drawings). Glue several together; glue a few leaning on others. Then put them on the shelves with sticky wax. Try cutting up an illustrated book catalog to get some of your favorite titles!

In genuine antiques there is a premium for small size. Breakfronts are the exception to this rule. These often-enormous pieces bring tens of thousands of dollars. Our Hepplewhite kit conversion is the perfect answer to the eternal question, "Where will I put all this stuff?" and for considerably less than $10,000.

Diagrams

Kit Renderings

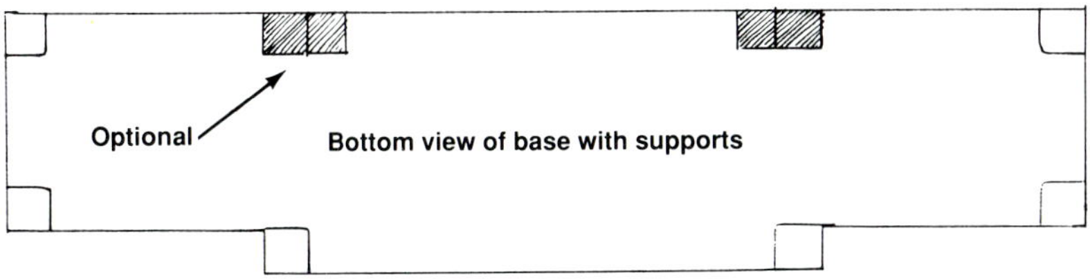

Diagrams

Kit Renderings

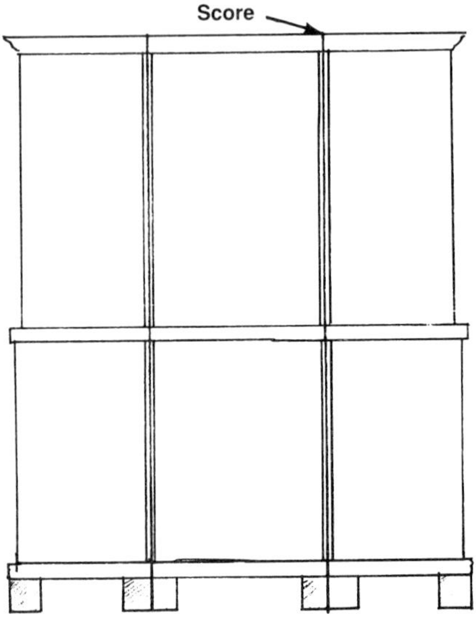

New feet & authentic scoring

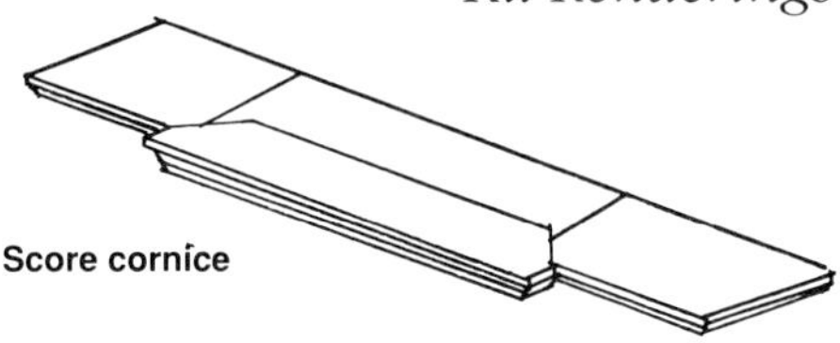

Score cornice

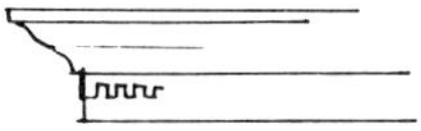

Optional dentil molding

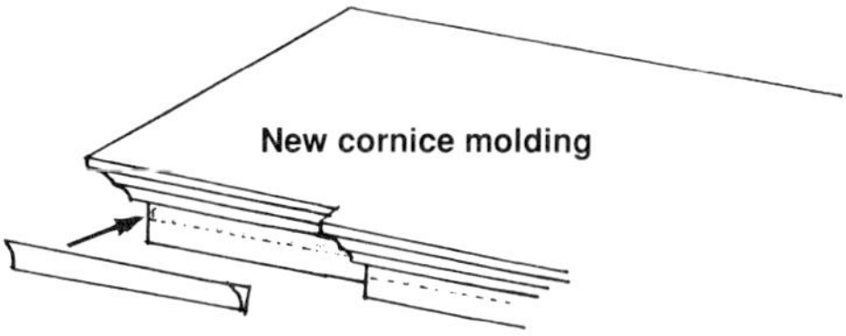

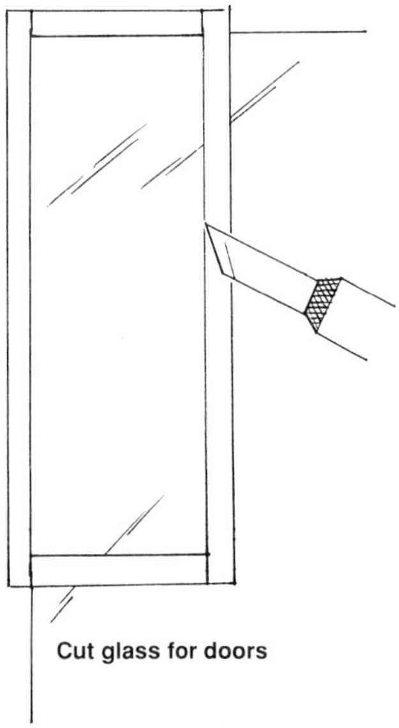

Cut glass for doors

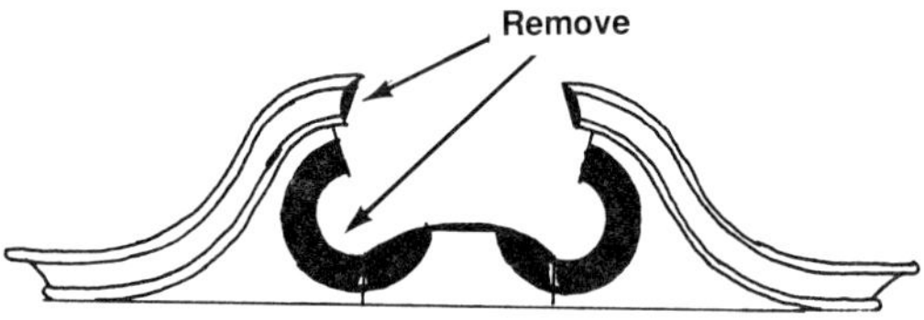

Re-cut cornice

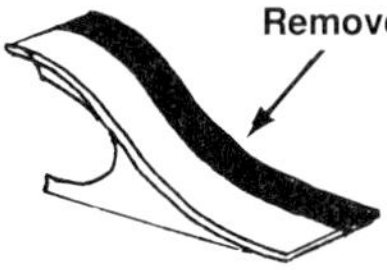

Cut pediment

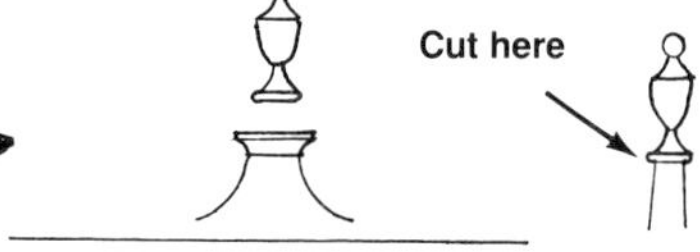

Finial on base

Bed post

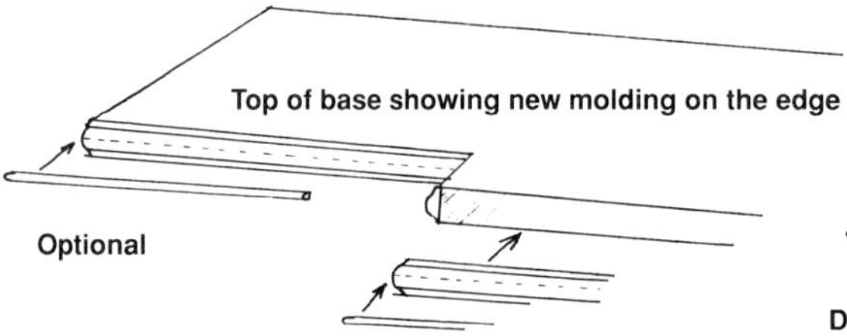

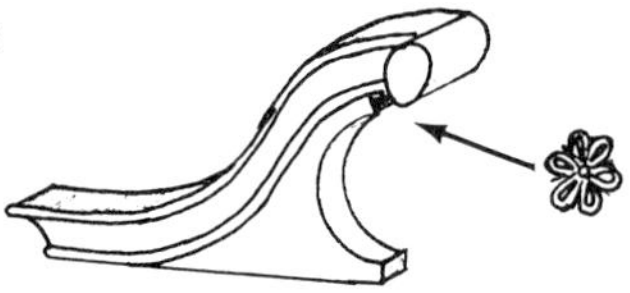

Dowel & doily

Diagrams

Kit Renderings

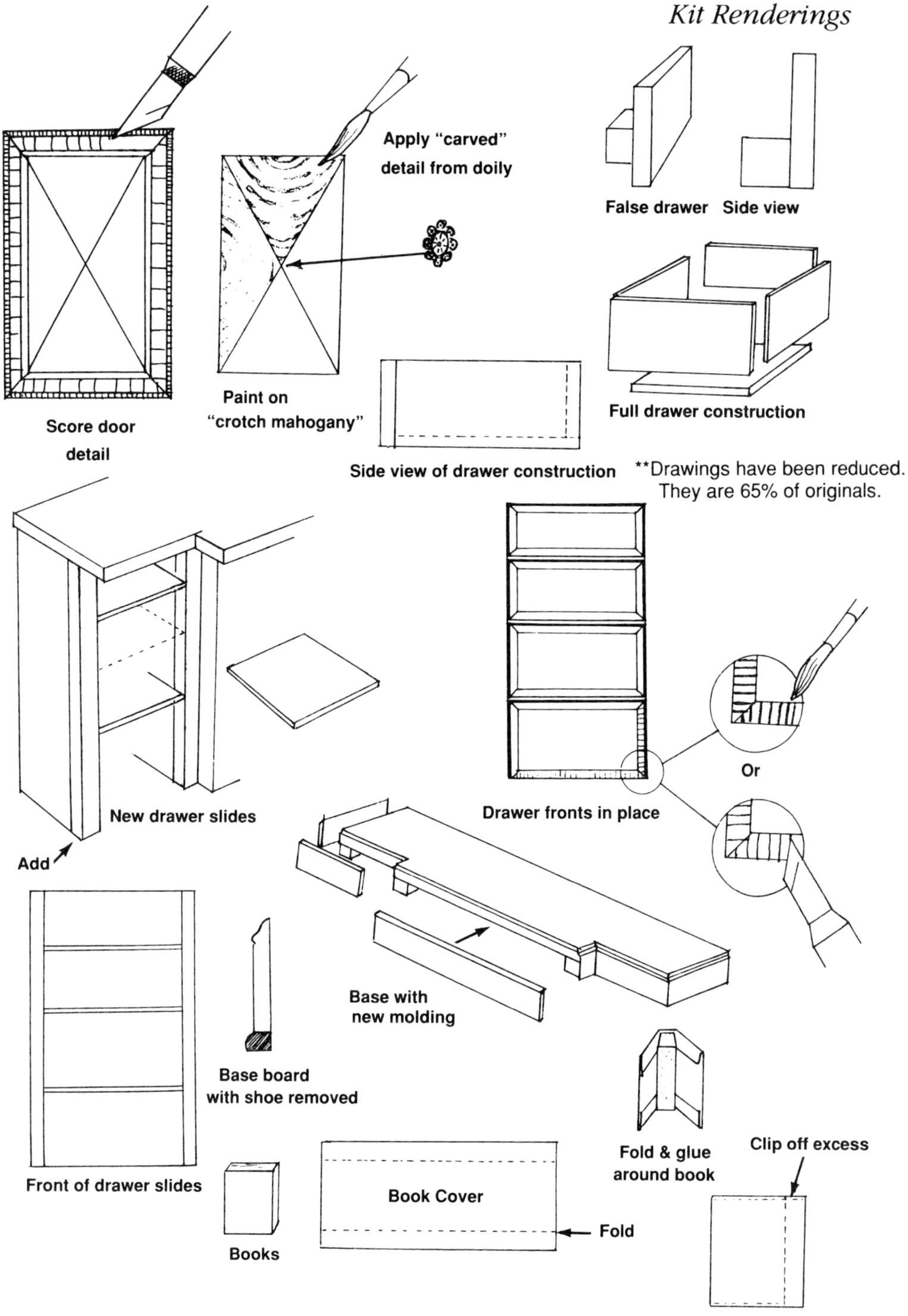

**Drawings have been reduced. They are 65% of originals.

Diagrams

Kit Renderings

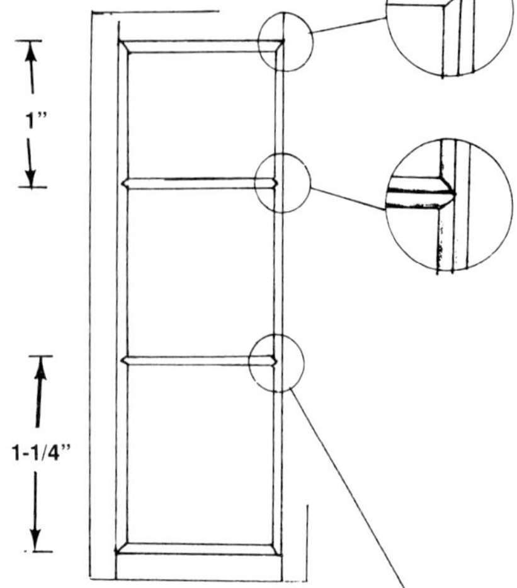

Front of doors, three-pane

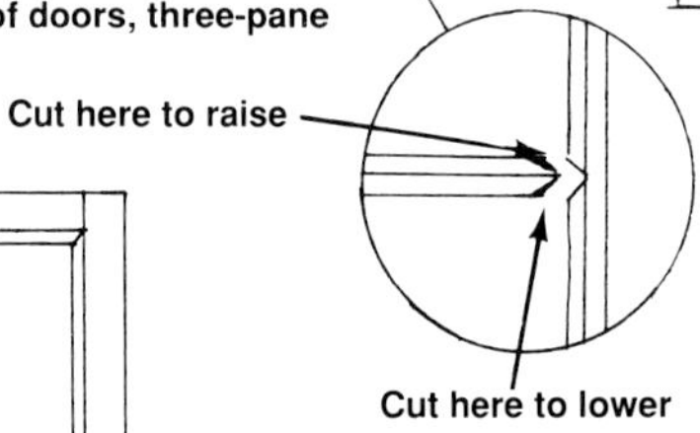

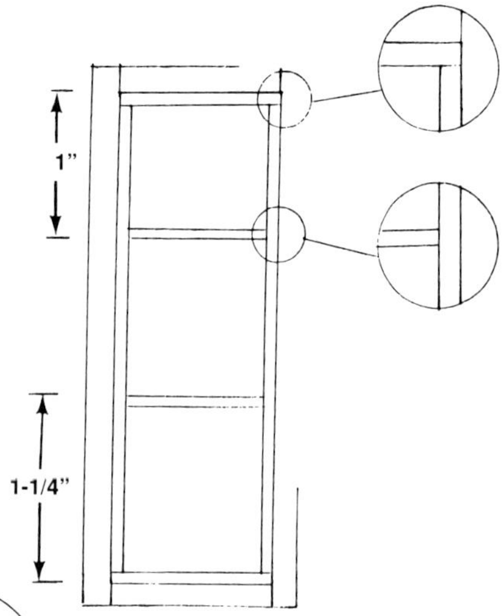

Back of doors, three-pane

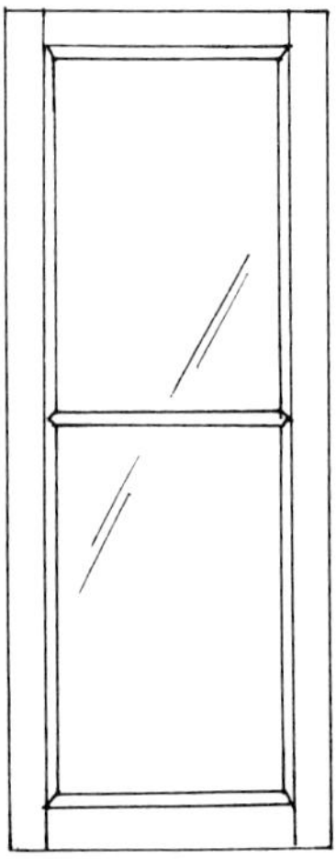

Two-pane option

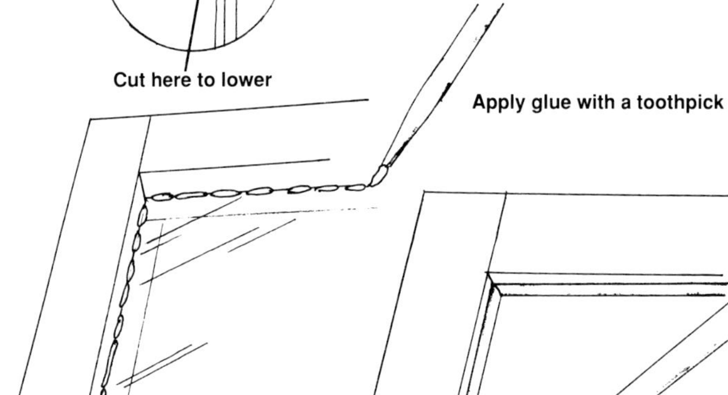

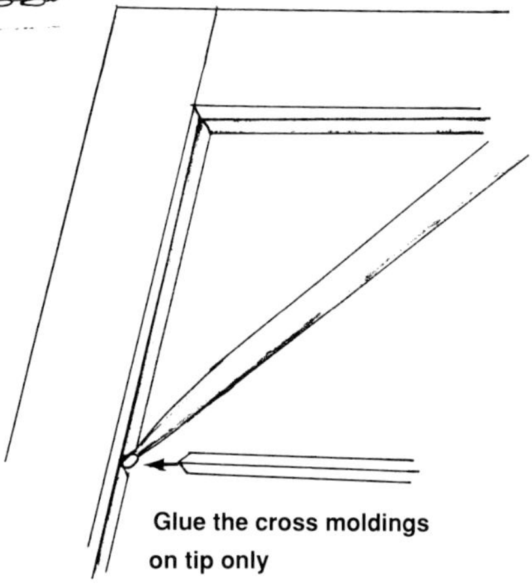

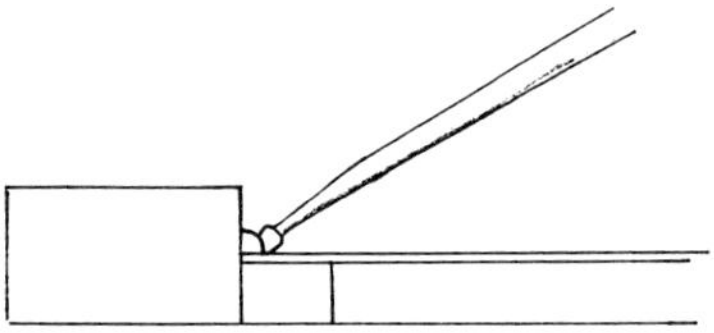

Side view glue

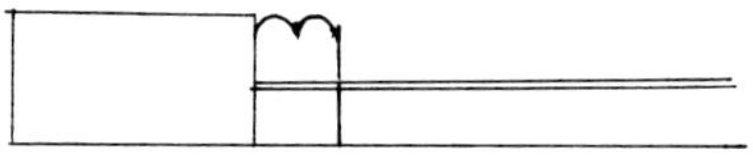

Side view, molding in place

An Inspired Hepplewhite

A three-drawer chest with all the right curves

THIS SERPENTINE CHEST is a Hepplewhite design inspired by the French. It is unusual for 18th century English pieces, since it has only three drawers. The French influence is the reason.

Once again House of Miniatures' #40050 Chippendale Serpentine chest is the basis for a beautiful "antique."

INSTRUCTIONS

Begin by removing the top section of parts #75 and 76. Be sure to cut above the drawer divider, so that it becomes a base for the top (see drawing). Once you have cut the upper sections off, cut the same amount of wood from the back, part #74, and assemble the case as shown in the kit instructions.

You will need to sand the top drawer slide a bit to flatten it and line it up with the sides and back. I found all of the slides to be a bit tight. Sand the edges slightly to make the kit easier to put together.

When the case is assembled, sand the canted edges down a bit more (see drawing). This is to make a larger ground for the new corners and legs.

Our new corners and legs are cut from 3/8" x 1/4" basswood. In the drawing you can see the basic steps involved. First draw the outline for the new corners on the 3/8" side of the basswood. Note that the back of the legs will also be cut out. You can see that here is where you need to be most careful. Use my template as a guide. Note that I have cut the feet 1/4" below the base. This is to leave room for the apron. Do this step for both corners.

The second step is to cut the angle of our new corners. Draw a triangle as a guide on top of your corners. The wide part of the triangle will be on the back (see drawing). Draw a guideline down the center of the front (see drawing). Cut toward this line on both sides. Be especially careful not to cut into the back line. This line must remain straight since it is glued against the canted corners on parts #75 and 76. The cut lines look fairly flat except for the area just below the top. This area dips in a bit more. Note that

MATERIALS

- House of Miniatures #40050 Chippendale Serpentine Chest
- 3/8" x 1/4" basswood
- 1/4" x 1/4" basswood
- 1/16" filler strip of basswood
- Delta Red Iron Oxide water based paint
- #S-8 round pulls, Susanne Russo
- #E-18 escutcheons, HB Brass; or #S-34 large French pulls and #S-35 large French escutcheons, Susanne Russo
- House of Miniatures mahogany finishing kit
- House of Miniatures clear finish
- Masking tape

The top of the chest (top photo) is pieced at the back, and its edges are cross-banded. The simulated grain shows different patterns on top, sides, and front.

The pattern of the simulated grain is clearly seen in this closeup. A vertical cut represents the veneer join in an "open-book" style. The front apron curves smoothly into the front leg.

the guideline will *not* be cut into. The final edge is fairly sharp and crisp.

The front apron is made from a 1/4" x 1/4" piece of basswood. First cut the serpentine to match the fronts of the drawers and slides (see drawing). Then cut the pattern as shown. I have adjusted the lines of the pattern slightly to more closely approximate the actual antique which I copied. The legs and the apron meet, and the curve flows from one to the other. Cut a shallow vertical line in the center as shown. This simulates the veneer join of the original. Now glue the corners and apron to the base. The front serpentine should flow into the corners in a smooth line. You will have a slight gap on the side behind the new corners. We will tend to this later.

Our back legs are made from a 3/8" x 1/4" piece of basswood. Draw the Hepplewhite legs on two sides, using my template. The wider measurement goes at the back. Cut off the excess wood as shown. Then cut a small amount from the inside of each back leg. This will create two slightly chunky back legs which will look deceptively thinner.

Our side apron joins the front and back legs and slightly repeats the front apron. When you have the two aprons completed, glue the aprons and back legs into place. Let these dry thoroughly before adding our filler strip.

The filler strip is a tiny strip of basswood cut into a vertical triangle, glued into place as shown and then sanded smooth. The base is cut at an angle to match the line of the apron. The antique appeared to have a piece of cross-banding at this point, so this filler will not look awkward.

The original top, part #73, has been recut to follow the line of the new corners. The easiest way to do this is to turn the base upside down on the top and trace a line following the new design. This requires that you push the top forward about 1/8" or more. This gap is filled with a strip of basswood the thickness of the top and slightly under 1/4" deep. I have included a template of my top to act as a guide. Some of you may prefer to cut an entirely new top which isn't pieced at the back. Period 18th century tops were often pieced at the back (never in the middle) and since we will simulate a line of cross-banding, the new addition will not be too obvious.

Our final cabinetwork is to simulate the cross-banding. I cut lines 1/8" from the edge at the front and sides, and cheated slightly at the back. Next score slight cuts all along as shown to simulate the cracks of old cross-banding.

Last, or first if you prefer, assemble the drawers. I cut a line down the center of the fronts to simulate the veneer join. This may be done before or after assembly. Whichever you choose, the three drawer fronts need to be lined up and *lightly* scored. If you cut too deep a line and it's incorrect, it is difficult to correct.

The drawers did not fit too well. I had to sand the top two drawers at the bottoms and sides to get them to slide into the openings. The lower drawer needed the sides sanded, and all three needed to have a good deal removed from the back so that they did not stick out.

Now our chest should be assembled and need only a light sanding to make it perfect for finishing. Begin with the drawers. Tape all three drawers together so that they may be treated as if they are one piece for finishing (see drawing).

Place a strip of masking tape on one side to prevent bleeding onto the other side. Quickly swirl the mahogany finish in the pattern shown in drawing and photo. As soon as this is done, remove the tape and set the drawers aside to dry; one full day is advisable. After this is done, reverse the process to give a beautiful book-matched veneer.

On the top, quickly swirl the "veneer" as shown, making much straighter grain than the drawer fronts. Work to the edge of the "cross-banding." The "cross-banding" is done with a combination of mahogany stain brushed on vertically and a few highlights brushed on with Red Iron Oxide water-based paint to fill in any spots or to emphasize the "'veneer."

Now finish the entire chest with House of Miniatures' clear finish. When this is dry, use the antiquer ("glaze" stain) to soften the lines and darken the back and undersides. This will come to the very edge of the outside finish. The legs are dark on the insides, *not mahogany color.* Since your clear finish will probably have overlapped a bit, you may need to "glaze" the edges a couple of times.

The actual antique had a drawer slide at the top. If you want a slide, use the unused divider, part #77. Cut the sides off as shown on my template and use it above the top drawer. Leave just enough of the sides on parts #75 and 76 so that the slide comes out smoothly. Use two brass sequin pins as pulls. Otherwise follow the same instructions.

The genuine antique was a transitional Chippendale to Hepplewhite chest. I used Susanne Russo's #S-8 round pulls, which give it a strong Hepplewhite look and are very much like the originals. The escutcheons are #E-18 from HB Brass. If you prefer a more Chippendale look, use Susanne Russo's #S-34 large French pulls and her #S-35 large French escutcheons.

These serpentine chests are rare and valuable. You have just created a wonderful museum piece for your miniature home.

Diagrams

Project diagrams may be photocopied for personal use

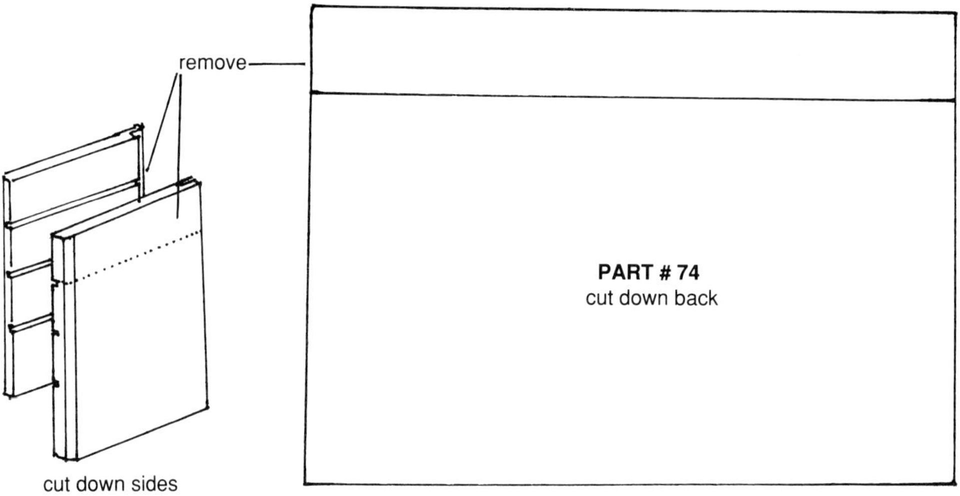

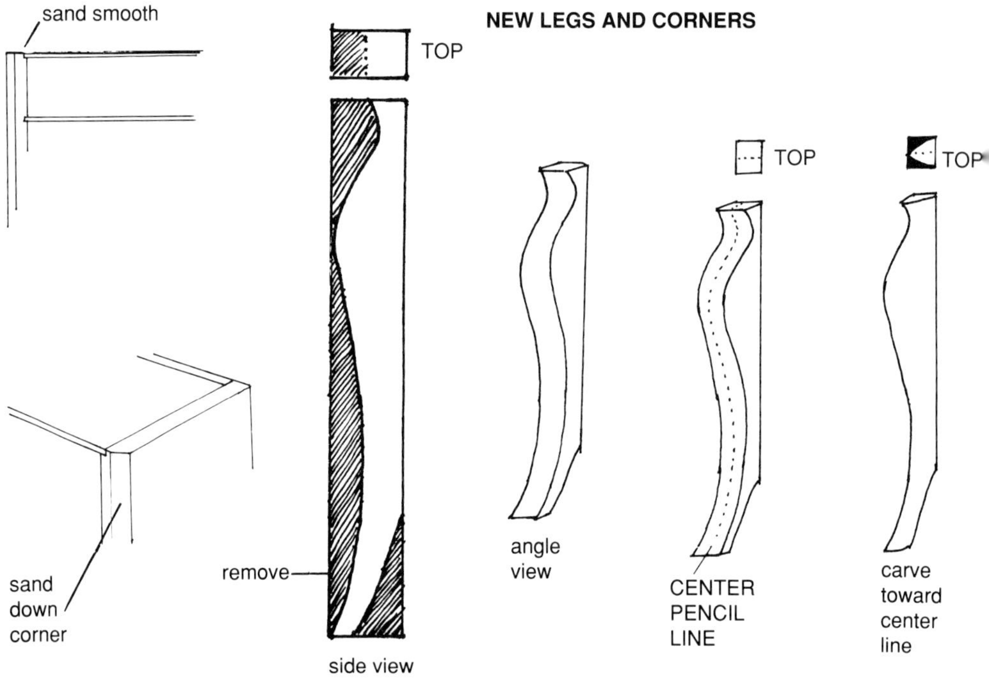

Diagrams

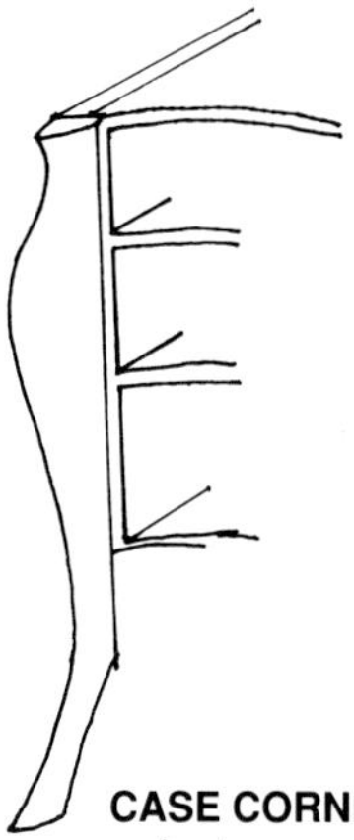

CASE CORNER
w. leg/corner attached

NEW APRON - top view

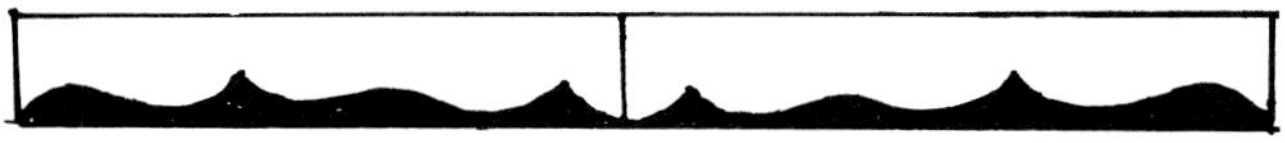

NEW APRON - front view

REAR LEG

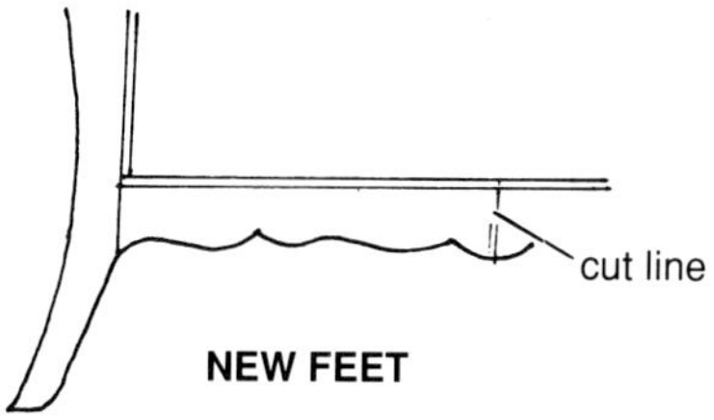

NEW FEET

TEMPLATE

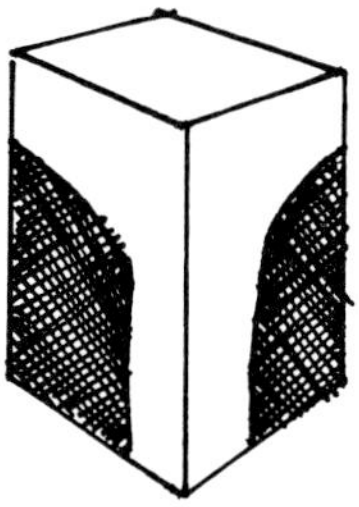

back view

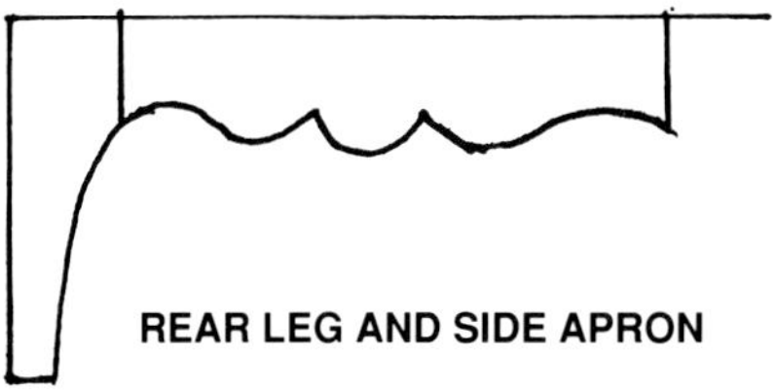

REAR LEG AND SIDE APRON

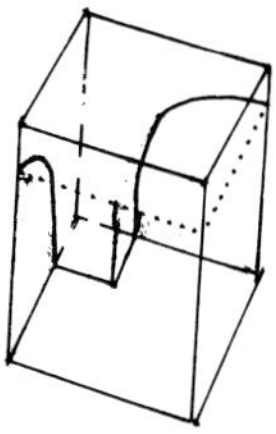

see-through angle view
cut out leg as shown

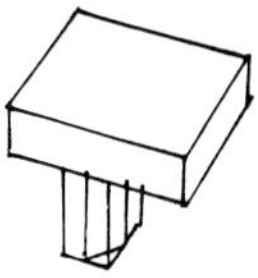

cut new angle
on rear leg

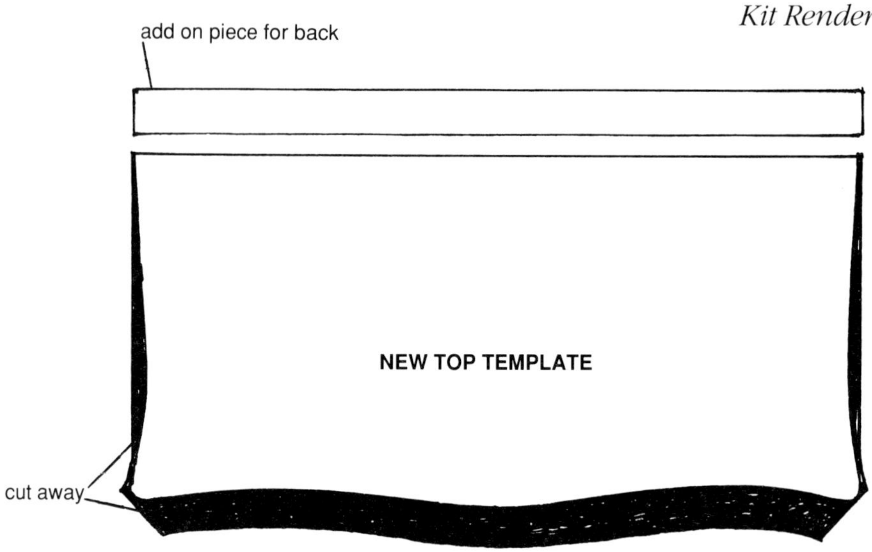

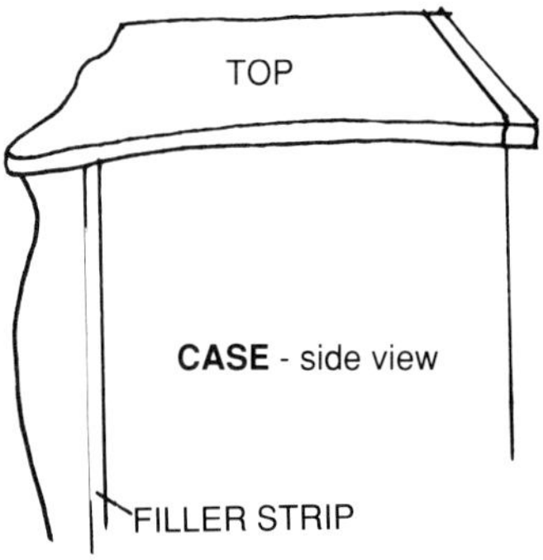

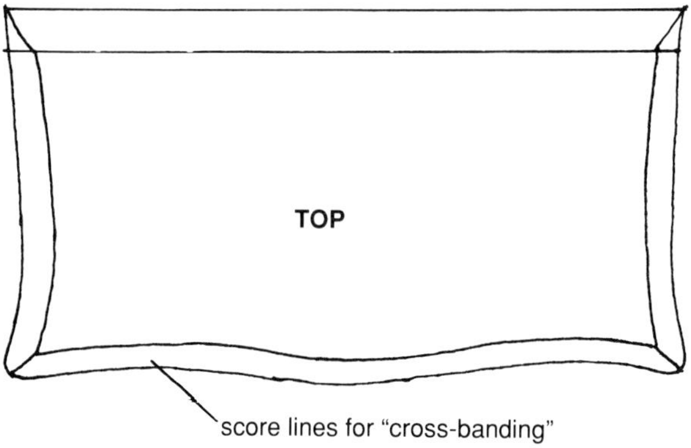

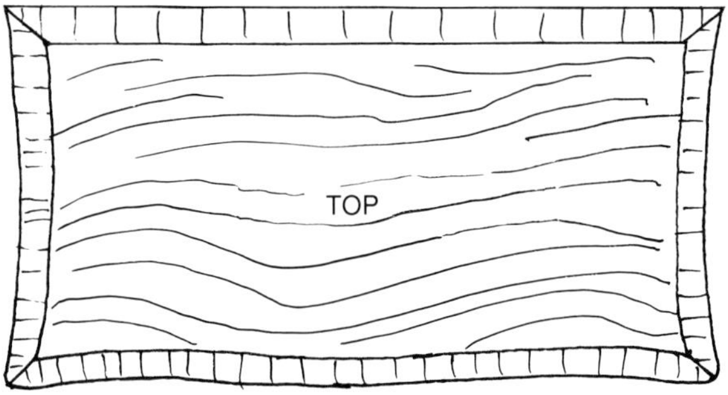

TOP GRAINING AND "CROSS BANDING"

Diagrams

FRONT

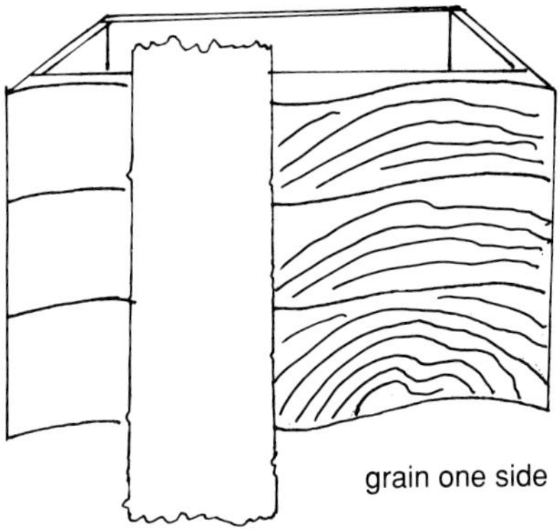

mask one side

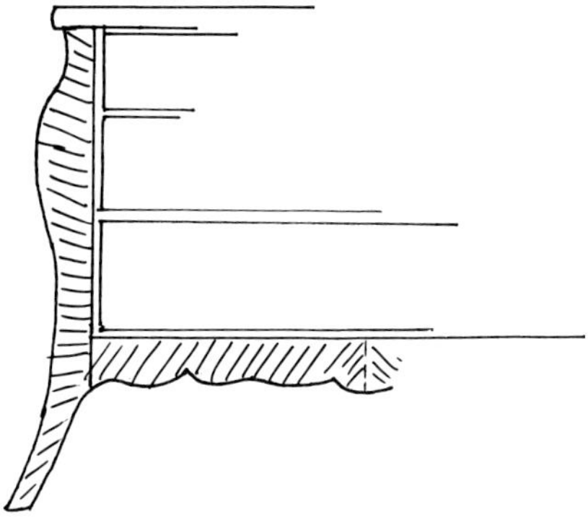

GRAIN PATTERN ON APRON & CORNER

DRAWER SLIDE

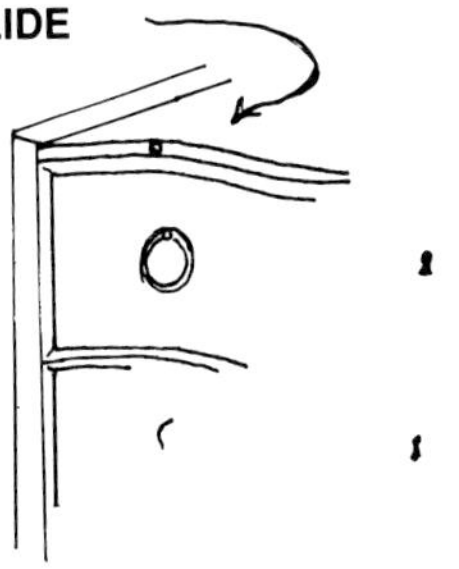

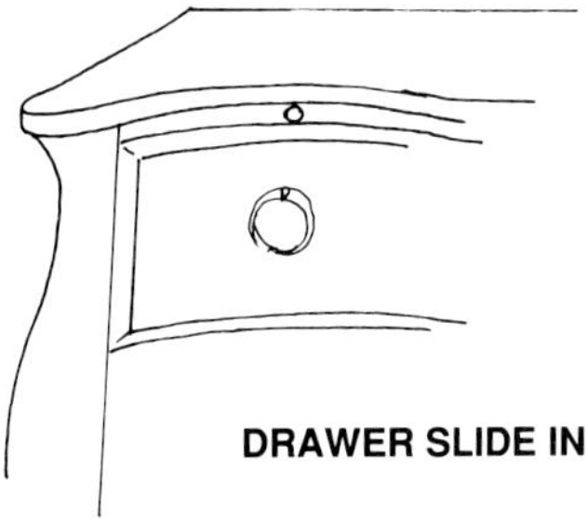

DRAWER SLIDE IN PLACE

Transform a Hepplewhite table into a work of art

SHERATON ELEGANCE

CRAFTMARK'S #40036 HEPPLEWHITE Serpentine table is an excellent starting point for creating an elegant Sheraton table. It also has great possibilities for a Chinese Chippendale table which you will see in a future installment.

INSTRUCTIONS

The wood in this kit was a bit rough. You will need to use a fine grade sandpaper to sand the outside edges of the sides, parts #3. Also sand the front edges of parts #4 and the outside edge of part #5. These parts form the case for the drawer and the base for the top and legs. There is no need to sand the top and bottom. The bottom should be a bit rough to simulate the rough appearance found under genuine antiques, and the top will have another top glued on top of it. Assemble these parts as instructed in steps 1 and 2 on your instruction sheet.

Unless you choose the painted version, the drawer front, part #11, will have a cross-banded "inlay." This "inlay" is very easy to make. Place a steel-edged ruler on the outside edge of the drawer. Run your X-Acto knife down this line, stopping short of the edge (see drawing). At the corner of each edge run a mitered line to indicate the end of each band of "inlay" (see drawing). Do this on all four edges.

At irregular intervals, run straight lines into the "inlay." These lines simulate the tiny cracks which occur on the genuine antiques (see drawing). If you cut these lines too deeply, the depth can be reduced with a light sanding.

Assemble the drawer as shown in steps 5 and 6 of Craftmark's instructions. Your drawer will probably be slightly larger then the opening in the base.

I had to sand the back quite a bit to make the drawer fit flush with the opening. If you want the drawer to slide in and out, the sides and bottom will need to be sanded as well. These kits have been in production for a number of years so it is common to find some minor ill-fitting parts.

I found the Hepplewhite tapered legs a bit chunky for such a small piece. I have replaced

MATERIALS

- Craftmark #40036 Hepplewhite Serpentine Table
- Four Houseworks #7009 porch spindles
- Craftmark's mahogany finishing kit
- Two #A2 oval pulls from HB Brass
- Inexpensive ballpoint pen
- X-Acto knife
- Fine sandpaper

them with new turned legs, #7009 porch spindles by Houseworks. These are a bit too long. To get the correct length, place the old legs (parts #7) next to the spindles and remove the excess at the narrow end of the spindles. These spindles will be used upside down to become our Sheraton legs.

When you have removed the excess length the leg will look a bit bottom heavy. With a small round file narrow the foot and thin the turning (see drawing). You will also slightly narrow the area just above the turning. The amount removed is very much to taste. The photography illustrates the alterations I chose to make. Note on the drawing I have narrowed the turning at both the top and the bottom.

Now glue the new legs into the corner slots of the drawer base (see drawing). Chances are good that the legs will be slightly different in length. Wait until the glue on the legs is set, then file off the excess length. Probably only one leg will require any adjustment.

If you choose, the top may remain the same as it comes in the kit. I have altered it to make it look more Sheraton. The new top design is similar to a large oval with four small circles on the edges. On the drawing you can see how this design is cut out of the existing top.

I have added corner "pockets" by pressing both ends of a commercial ballpoint into the wood. Press the large end in first (see drawing), then push the other end (with the point retracted) into the wood. This will give a wonderful sculpted look for our mahogany version. Should you choose the painted option, do not "sculpt" these circles into the wood. Follow the basic shape in the drawing, but leave the top perfectly flat. Painted versions rarely had sculpted pockets.

You may now glue the top onto the base and legs. Be sure the pockets are over the new turned legs. They will be slightly larger than the tops of the legs.

If you are making the mahogany version, it is

best to stain all the parts before you construct the table. Note how I have swirled the stain on to get a crotch mahogany effect. This needs to be done very rapidly. Do the sides and back the same way. The legs have only a slight "grained" look since care would have been taken to select wood with very slight grain pattern on the originals. The drawer front has a swirled mahogany front with "satinwood" cross-banding. To get this effect use the clear stain on the "cross-banding" before you swirl the mahogany "grain." You may like the satinwood effect, but I found it not entirely satisfactory. Were I to do it over again I would brush the mahogany stain on the "cross-banding" as well as the front.

On the top edge brush the stain vertically to simulate a cross-banded edge. This may be further reinforced by creating the cracking effect seen on the drawer cross-banding. Should you choose to try it, this needs to be done very carefully. The X-Acto knife should not cut into the top edge at all. You will get an unpleasant edge which will be very noticeable when you apply the "glaze" (antique) stain. I omitted the cracks. You may judge for yourself if they are necessary (see photograph).

After you have stained the table, use the clear sealer on all parts except the underside. This will be brown, painted with the "glaze" stain. When the clear sealer is completely dry, brush the edges and crevices with the "glaze" stain. Wipe it off so that a tiny bit remains in the deeper spots. This will give a wonderful old effect. You will also want to stain the underside at this time.

If you have chosen the painted version you

Diagrams

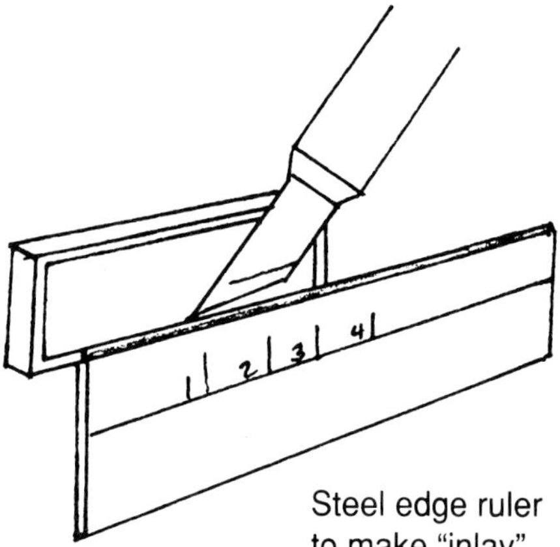

Steel edge ruler
to make "inlay"

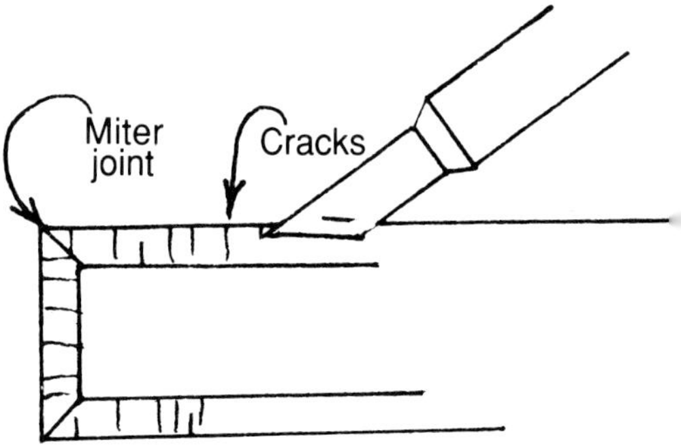

Cut cracks on "cross-banding"

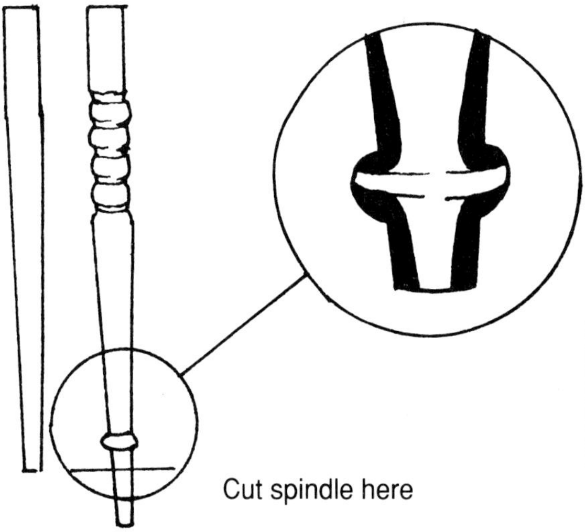

Narrow foot
and lower leg

Cut spindle here

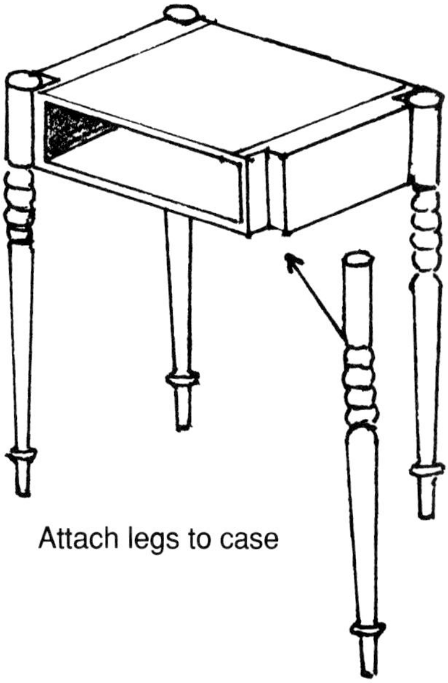

Attach legs to case

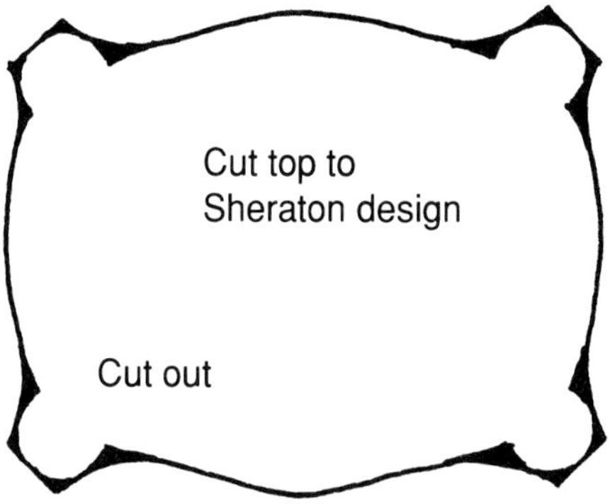

Diagrams

Kit Renderings

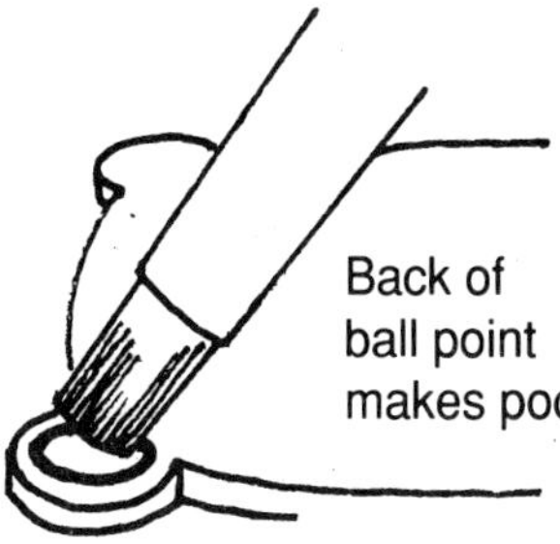

Back of ball point makes pocket

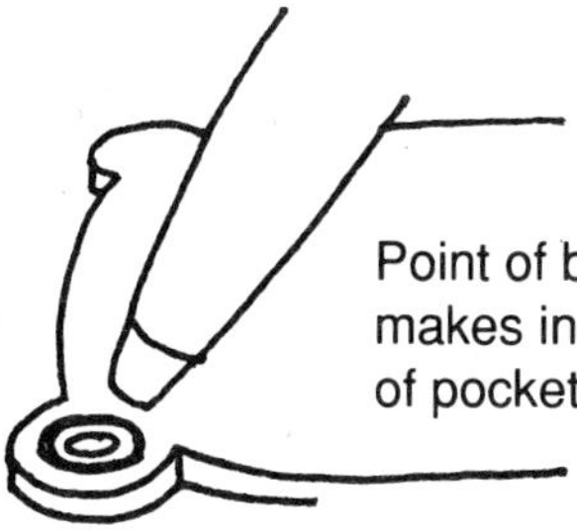

Point of ball point makes inside circle of pocket

Gold lines

Pale green

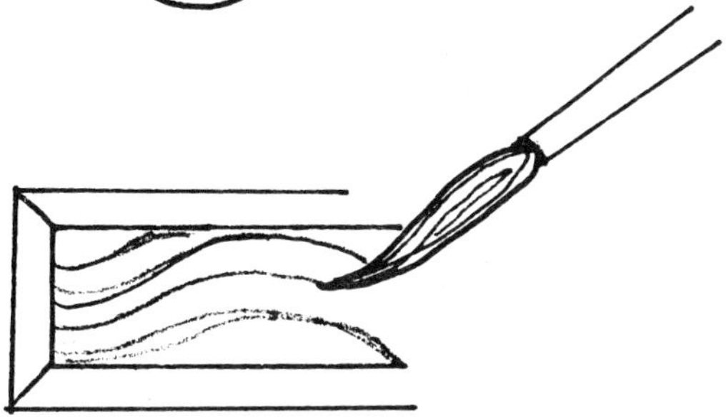

Swirl grain on drawer front

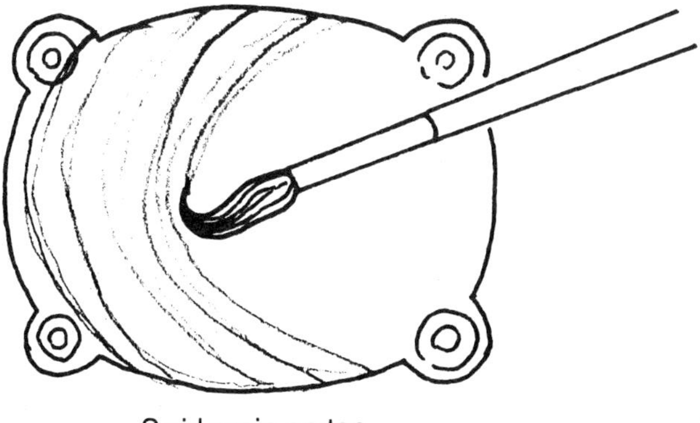

Swirl grain on top

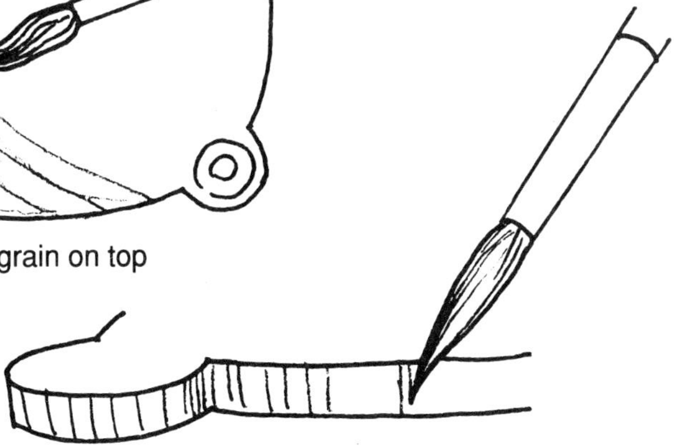

Gold line

Paint cross-banding on edge of top

Diagrams

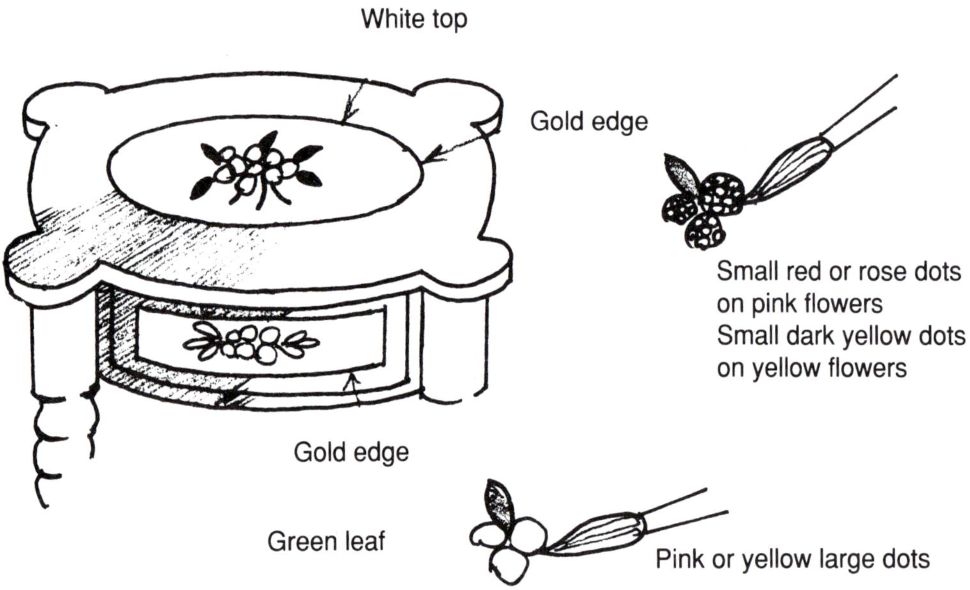

should be aware that there are only three high-style colors: white, black, and dark green. The paint may also be done on "satinwood" which would be a clear finish over the basswood. Other colors are seen, but they are usually country versions.

I have drawn a typical painted version to be your guide. This may be adapted as you see fit. The central oval top may be white as a contrast to the dark green or black. The oval may be just a gold line on the dark color. The flowers will be in natural colors with a mixture of yellow and rose colors. I have made a special drawing detailing how to get flower effects easily.

Unless your center oval is white it is best to stay away from blue flowers. They won't be seen against dark colors. I have drawn typical designs, but a little research can turn up many others.

I recommend gold or light green and gold acanthus leaves painted on the upper part of each turning (see drawing). Paint a gold line around the lower turning as well. Follow the instructions on my drawing.

I have left the drawer pulls until last. I used HB Brass's #A2 Federal brasses. You may prefer their #A5 Sheraton brass. I used their #E18 escutcheon; #E16 is equally correct. Any of these combinations look fine on the mahogany version. If you do a painted version you will need to be a bit more creative for pulls. Most painted tables used knobs rather than pulls. To make knobs use two tiny brass nails like the one provided in the kit. As a backplate you may use two of the smallest gold sequins you can find; or use the backplates from HB Brass's Chippendale bail pulls, #H9, H38, or H41. Remember you are using only the backplate of those brasses. The pull will be the two small brass nails.

There your have it! You now have a beautiful Sheraton table, c.1800, probably produced in New York or Boston in the most up-to-date London style. Whichever version you choose you will have an heirloom that will please many generations to come.

Both these chairs, the Sheraton at left and the French Empire, came from the same chair kit design.

Two Classical Chairs

Recapture revival elegance of 1800

CRAFTMARK'S #40044 LYRE Back Chair is a good beginning for two fine classical chairs. These two chairs are expressions of the classical revival of the late 18th and early 19th centuries. Our Sheraton chair reflects a more frivolous and less academic approach to classical style. While its profile is remarkably like ancient Greek chairs, the back and seat are lighter and more whimsical. This lightness is a product of chairmakers guilds, which understood exactly how delicate a chair could be and yet remain strong.

Our French chair is influenced by architects. These chairs were designed to be a part of architectural schemes. There is a seriousness to these elegant designs that is both academic and practical. Both of these designs are enjoying a much deserved return to fashion.

INSTRUCTIONS

Our first chair is a late Sheraton chair c. 1800 that could be either English or American. At this date many British cabinetmakers, such as Duncan Phyfe, had emigrated to America. They eliminated the provincial lines of earlier American furniture and produced some of the finest furniture ever made in this country.

Begin by reshaping parts #60, the rear legs. My drawing shows the cuts to make to thin and sharpen the lines of this part. In the front view you can also see that the legs are made to taper inside up to the seat line. This taper lightens the chair and makes it look less heavy. All period chairs of this style have tapered legs.

We need to treat the front legs, parts #62, in the same manner. Again your taper should not

The Sheraton chair's back bears a gold accent in the center.

The top rail of the French Empire chair flows smoothly into its back.

go into the seat line. Should you make this mistake, your legs will curve inward when glued. While you are adjusting the front legs, add the circle seen on the drawing and in the photo. Push the end of a ballpoint, point removed, into the leg in the location shown. This circle is optional, but is often found on quality chairs.

Round the fronts of parts #62, the front legs, and the tops of parts #61, the side rails. There is a slight rounding where parts #61 meet parts #60 (see drawing) but most of the front edge of parts #60 is flat. Remove a small section of the back of part #61, the side rails. This will match up with the new line of the back as shown on the drawing. You may now glue parts #60, 61, and 62 together to complete the sides.

Our seat is a piece of cardboard cut the size of the seat, part #64. Bend it into a flattened U to match the line of the seat rail, part #61. Glue the foam seat on top of the cardboard, then upholster the seat. I used a piece of black felt underneath to finish it off, but I didn't install it until everything else was completed. Cut a new front rail from either 1/8" half round moulding or 1/8" double bead moulding. I used the latter. This is glued in front of the new seat and slightly under to give a rounded line to the front seat (see drawing and photo). At the rear of the seat you may use a simple 1/16" strip of basswood to complete the seat. This is optional since it is hardly seen, but it will give a stronger connection for the chair.

Our new back is based on a design taken from *The London Book of Prices*, dated 1808. This was a pricing guide for cabinetmakers. Make the bottom and top rails from 1/16" double bead moulding. My rails are 1" wide, but the width will vary depending on the thickness of the upholstery you choose. I temporarily taped the seat and sides together to get the sizes I needed. You may even want to glue the seat to the sides at this time. Then you can measure the width of the back.

When you have cut these new pieces, glue them in the locations shown. The lower rail will rest just where the new curve that we have cut begins to reverse (see drawing and photo). My rails are 7/16" apart, but I suggest you locate them visually. When these two are in place, cut a diagonal piece of the same double bead moulding as shown in Step 1 of the drawing. In Step 2 you can see that the X of the back is created by cutting two other pieces of the same moulding and gluing them in place as shown. I covered the join with a gold foil period which I got from a dime store set of gold foil alphabets. These have gum that has to be moistened to be used. Don't buy the self-stick alphabets. White glue doesn't adhere very well to self-stick glue. We will use more of these on our French chair. Paint the foil with Ceramcoat Red Iron Oxide waterbased paint. There are also some good model airplane enamels that match our mahogany color very well.

Our upper rail is 1/8" dowel turned as shown. I used a small file to turn the design. I think my rail looks a bit heavy-handed, but I didn't want to use a lathe, since not many of you will have

MATERIALS

- Craftmark #40044
  Lyre Back Chair Kit
- 1/8" double bead molding
- 1/16" double bead molding
- 1/16" basswood strip (optional)
- 1/8" dowel
- Set of gold foil alphabet
- Cardboard
- Ballpoint pen
- Craftmark mahogany stain and clear finish
- Ceramcoat Red iron Oxide waterbased paint

Add for French option:
- Two Houseworks #7009 porch spindles
- 1/4" dowel

one. You will need to angle the edges since the sides come in at an angle.

You may now stain all the parts with Craftmark mahogany stain and clear finish. If you want a purely English chair, stain the chair black to represent ebony.

Our French empire chair c. 1800 is a bit less work, but equally interesting. The only alteration on the back legs and uprights (parts #60) is to cut the inside taper to thin the back legs. You may want to round the top edge to gain smoother line when you install the dowel across the back (see drawing).

The seat is a box seat, which should have a very hard line. I glued both of parts #63 together and glued the cardboard base and foam cushion, part #65 together. French chairs ought to be a bit wider than the kit seat. I suggest you widen the seat slightly by gluing two small rectangles of cardboard the height of the seat to either side. I did not do this on my chair, but you can see proper proportions on my drawing.

There are two alternations to the side rail, part #61. First straighten the curve as shown on the drawing, then cut the sides into an angle. These two new rails can be glued near the front of the box seat. You may now cut a new thin front rail which will square up the front. This shows well in the drawing and the photo. I can't give exact sizes since everyone's will vary slightly.

The new front legs are cut from two Houseworks #7009 porch spindles. French Empire legs are rather plain. I cut a slight recess just about $1/8$" from the end and glued gold foil cut from my letters (see drawing). These were slightly short. Glue a small patch to the rear. No one will notice it. If you are feeling ambitious, you can sand the legs down to make them thinner. The legs are somewhat heavy as they come, but not overly awkward.

The new back begins with a $1/4$" dowel with notches cut out so that the rail seems to flow into a circle (see drawing). The width will vary, depending on upholstery and whether you choose to widen the seat as I suggested. The drawing shows what to do. My upholstered back is $1/2$" tall. It is a simple piece of cardboard bent slightly round, with a rectangle of foam glued to it. Upholster it to match the seat and glue it below the cushion.

Our "ormalou" circles are periods and circles cut from semi-colons and exclamation marks in our gummed foil letters. Place these as shown. This chair should be stained mahogany. The color may be quite dark if you like.

Diagrams

SHERATON CHAIR

PART #60
remove
shaded
areas

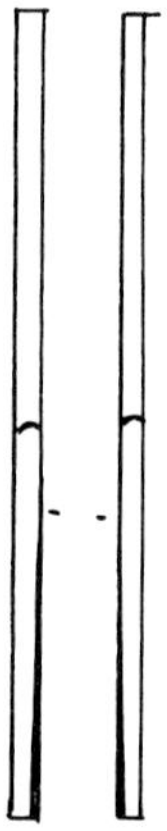

PARTS #60
front view
taper inside legs

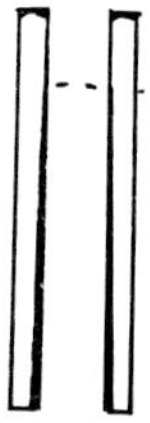

PARTS #62
front view
taper inside legs

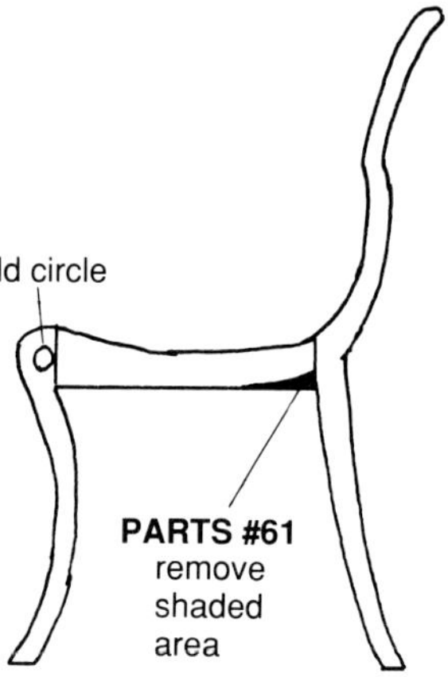

PARTS #61
remove
shaded
area

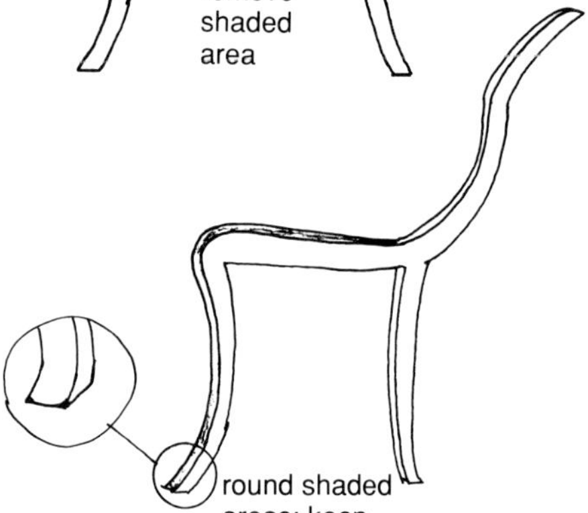

round shaded
areas; keep
others flat

bend cardboard seat;
glue sponge seat

BACK RAIL TURNING

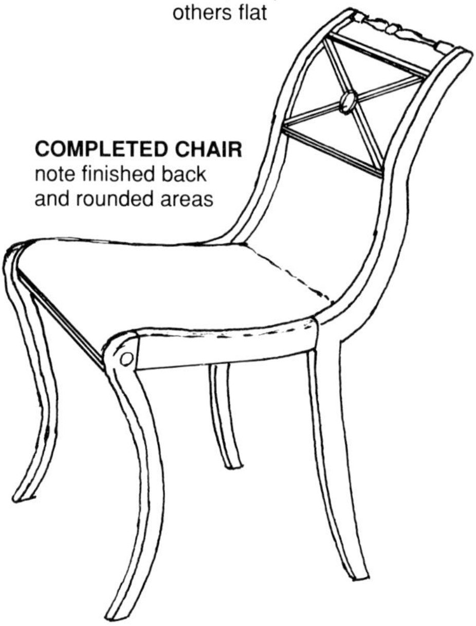

COMPLETED CHAIR
note finished back
and rounded areas

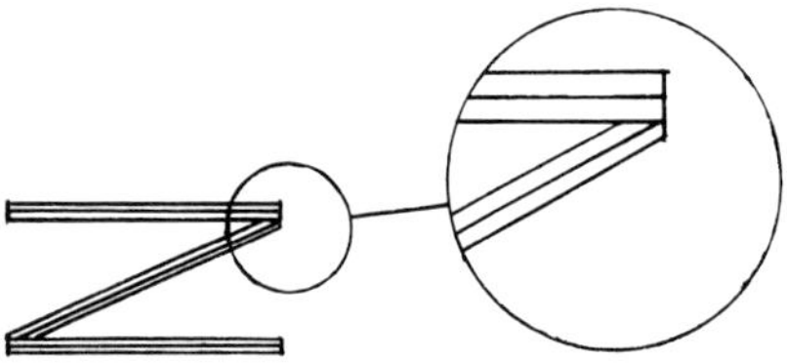

CHAIR BACK - Step 1

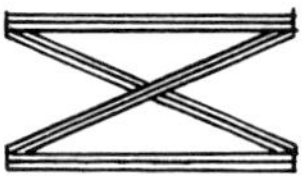

glue gold foil
circle to center

CHAIR BACK - Step 2

Diagrams

FRENCH EMPIRE CHAIR

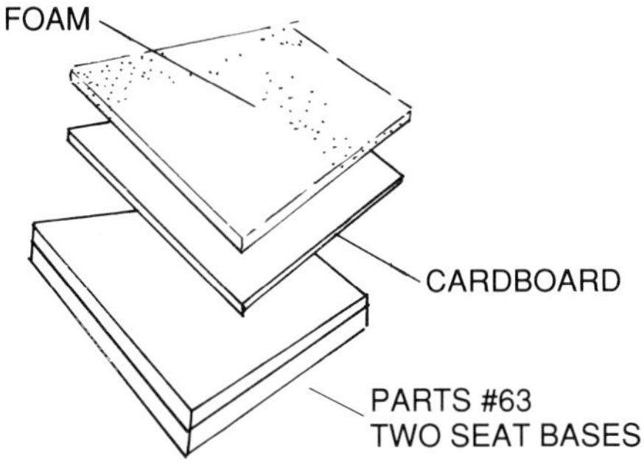

NEW SEAT

PART #61 - side view
remove shaded area

PARTS #61 - top view
remove shaded areas

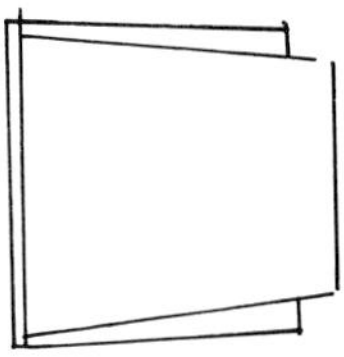

SEAT - top view
with sides and
new front in place

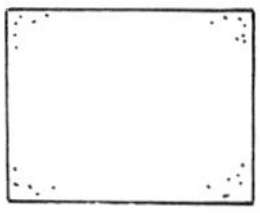

CARDBOARD BACK
cover with foam

MAKING BACK RAIL

HOUSEWORKS #7009
PORCH SPINDLES

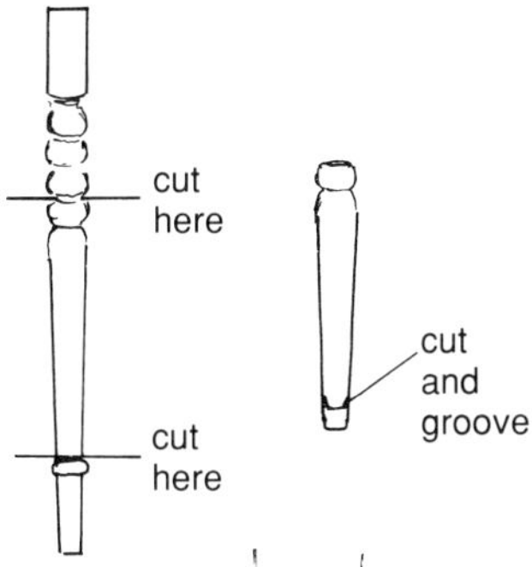

cut gold
foil letters

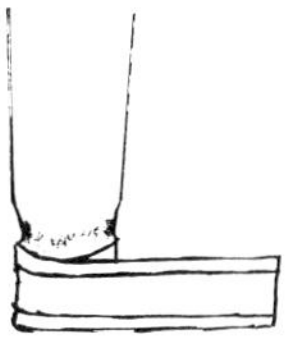

glue and wrap
gold foil to foot

FRENCH EMPIRE CHAIR
with gold foil circles in place

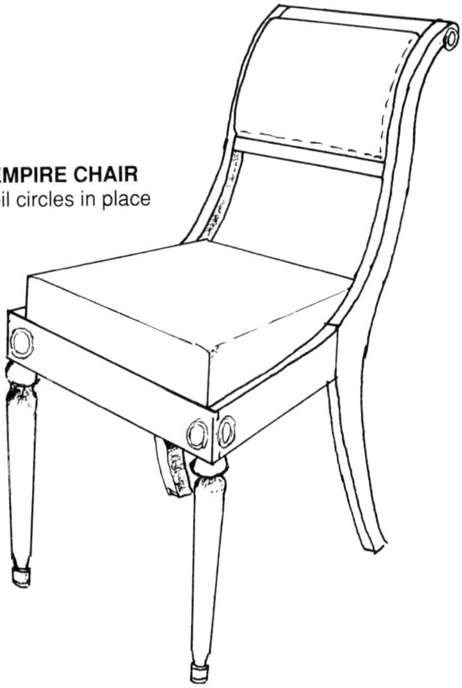

An Adam-Sheraton Commode

Create an 18th Century masterpiece

PHOTOS BY DARLA EVANS

INTERMEDIATE

Housework's Lingerie chest is a perfect jumping off point for a fine Adam-Sheraton commode.

Let's begin with parts #1 and #2, the sides. Remove the center panel of both sides (see drawing). Be sure to leave the recessed sections where the drawer slides are placed. When you have cut these two sections, assemble the center drawer section as shown in the kit instructions. You will, of course, have only three drawer openings instead of the original seven. Set aside this section and the two remaining sides for later. Note the four "sides" are interchangeable, but do have a proper front and back.

Now we will cut two new parts, the top and base. I used 1/8" basswood. On my drawing you can see the base is slightly smaller than the top. Be sure the angle of the curves correspond. This is important since the new doors will have the same curve. I cut a guideline 1/16" in from the edges around the top, and used a small jar as a guide for the semi-circle. I cut these lines with an X-Acto knife, but they may be penciled in if you have a steady painting hand. We will use these two parts shortly.

Using my template as a guide, cut a new back for the commode. Once you have this piece you may

begin assembly of the body. Note that the drawer section will have a space behind it and the back. This will not show outside. Place your drawer section directly in the center of the new base and glue into place. Next, glue the sides and back in place. The back will be flush with the sides, glue it into the recess provided, and on top of the new base. At this point you will probably need some adjustment. You may need to even the back and sides a bit. The exploded view should show these and the next steps.

You may now attach your new top. I designed the top to fit flush with the back. This is not correct period design, but is easy to line up and place. If you want to be authentic add 1/16" to the back of the new top. This would have allowed the top to fit fairly flush with the wall when a chair rail was used.

Our new doors are cut from 1/16" basswood. Rather than curve the wood itself, I decided to cut a vertical concave into the wood. Use my templates as a guide for size, but remember you will probably have to make some adjustments. One adjustment you will certainly have to make is to angle the doors near the drawers. This is because the doors are set at an angle. You will also need to make a stop for the door. (see drawing) Any small piece of wood will do. If the doors are to be opened, use a small piece similar to the one in my drawing.

Cut an oval in the center of the two doors. (see drawing) This is a painting guide. Don't make the oval smaller, but you may increase the size. Note I have also cut diagonals on each of the doors. These

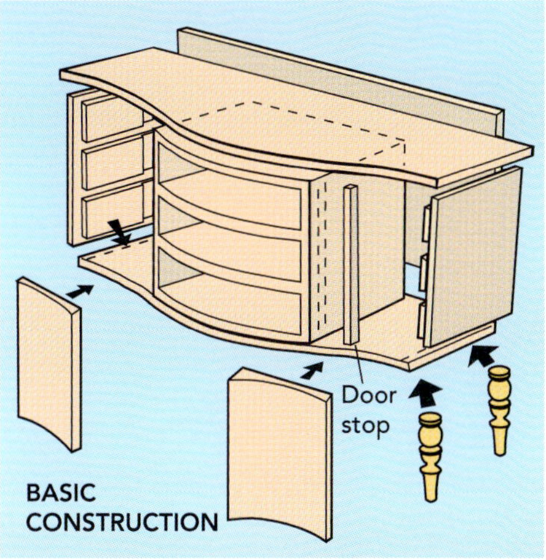

are optional. Others would have used a sheet of veneer and painted the design on top of that. This is your choice.

Our legs are made from two sections of turnings by Tiny Turnings. I cut six sections from Tiny Turnings #1000 turnings. Note I cut the two outer rings off. Then I used six sections of Tiny Turnings #4000, removing the lower turnings and cutting flush with the next small turning. (see drawings) These are then glued on top of one another to look like six single legs. The effect is not entirely correct, but is fairly close to my antiques. Glue these in place as shown in the photographs. Pay particular attention to getting the legs straight. The

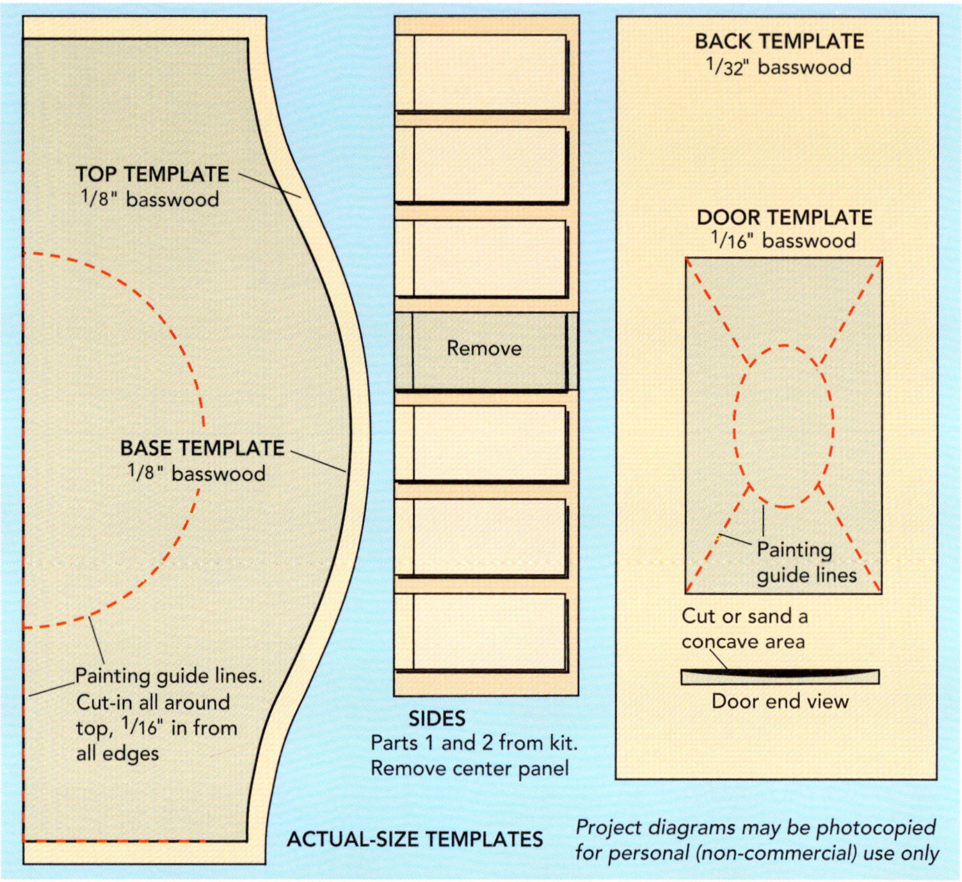

Materials Needed

Houseworks Bowfront Lingerie Chest
Sheet 1/8" basswood
Sheet 1/16" basswood
#1000 turnings by Tiny Turnings
#4000 turnings by Tiny Turnings
Water-based or enamel paints
Deft clear finish
Gold enamel
#S-8 Round drawer pulls by Susanne Russo (now at Black Diamond Designs)
#S-18 Small round escutcheons by Susanne Russo (see Shoppers' Guide)
or
#A-1 brasses by HB Brass
#E-16 escutcheons by HB Brass

antiques occasionally have warped legs, but I don't suggest trying for that effect.

Now comes the fun part, the painting. One glance at my commode and many of you will be put off attempting such an "ambitious" design. Now look closer. All the painting is a series of simple formulas.

To paint the bows seen on the top and the upper parts of each wreath on the doors begin with a simple "x". Next close the ends of the "x" with curved lines, then paint two more curved lines to be the ends of the bows. (see drawings) These lines may be all the same size, but it will look more like fabric if the lines vary in thickness.

The bellflowers are short strokes with the brush. Note that the second step is two more of the exact strokes. (see drawings) On the doors you will paint pairs of bellflowers on the four diagonal lines, or on a diagonal should you not cut these lines. The bellflowers are also used as a border for the semi-circle on the top.

The wreaths, and the backgrounds for the flowers

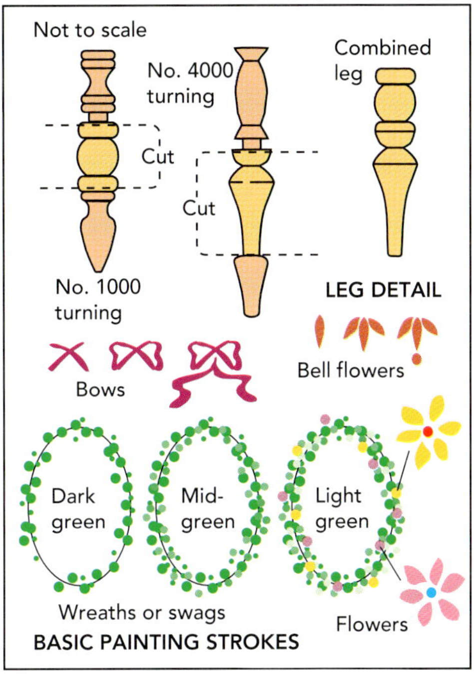

are a series of untidy dots in two or three shades of green. The drawing gives you the basic idea. Do not use pure or dark green. It will overpower the rest of the design. I used three shades of a muddy yellow green as you can see. Note that the design in the semi-circle has a few leaves floating around, this is typical of period design and would not have bothered the 18th century eye.

The flowers in the ovals and the ones on top are a series of four or five dots with a contrasting color in the center, usually a dull orange. My white "flowers" are simply dots of white on the green. Note in the photographs that the swags on the drawers have flowers of several different colors which are simply dots of color. As the photograph shows, many of these flowers float in space. This is correct for the period. The effect is surprisingly grand for such a simple technique.

I used a medium dull green for my trim color and a pale blue on the background color. This is typical of late Adam design as copied by Thomas Sheraton in the 1790s. Should you prefer a design from the earlier period, say 1770, replace the green with pale grey or dull pale blue, lighten the background blue and you are correct.

I used Deft clear finish over the entire design, then added gold touches on the legs. While I used water-based paints for all my painting, you will get equally good results with enamels.

Use a dark brown stain on the back and underside for an "antique" piece. For a commode which exists in an 18th century setting, paint the back and underside with a slight mahogany wash.

I used Suzanne Russo's #S-8 round Sheraton pulls and her #S-18 small round escutcheons. These are now available from Black Diamond designs. You may use the pulls included in the kit or #A-1 pulls by HB Brass, and #E-16 escutcheon by HB Brass is a good companion with either of the latter pulls.

A Capital Pair

Two chairs recall White House history

ONE OF OUR chairs is the result of combining two different chairs from the original White House. I took the lines from one and the painted detail from the other. The second chair is based on a French design c. 1620. A version of this is from a similar White House chair that dates from the Lincoln era. This is our second attempt at altering the chairs in House of Miniatures #40007 chair kit

INSTRUCTIONS

Begin the first chair with two parts #12, the chair sides. Remove 1/16" from the base of each foot. Narrow the lower parts of both front and back legs (see drawing). Square the "join" of the side rail and the front legs as shown. Leave the curve on the rear legs (see drawing).

I re-shaped the back by cutting a notch in the wood to enhance the classical line. I also lowered the back rail by 1/16" (see drawing).

Our final alteration to parts #12 is to taper the *inside* legs slightly for a narrower, more graceful look. Please note: the edges taper *inside*. You may want to pencil a mark where the seat will be glued so that you can't accidentally assemble these parts backward.

Our new seat may be constructed using the template. I used 1/16" thickness, but 1/8" will work as well. Our new front and back are just under 1/4" high. The thickness is just under 1/8". You will have to adjust these measures slightly so that the seat front and back square up with the sides. Now glue all this together and set aside.

Our new back is basswood, 1/2" x 1½" x 1/32" thick. Use your X-Acto knife to cut a line 1/8" all around for your painting guide. Play with this piece, bending it back and forth to get a graceful curve in the back.

On the back uprights, I removed a sliver of wood at an angle behind the new back (see drawing) to help the back retain its shape. This is so slight it can hardly be seen, but it will give you a much better bond. I assembled the chair

These chairs, seen opposite, were inspired by historic White House chairs.

The gold design on the back, above, may be replaced by the visible yellow base coat, outlined with black.

Formal tassels mark the seat corners. India ink was used for the pinstripe edging.

seat and sides (parts #12), then glued the new back between the uprights, placing a weight on the back to hold the curve in place until the back dried.

The lower splat is cut from one of the legs of the other chair, since the front legs will be removed from our second chair. I cut the thickness down to 1/16". Should you plan to make a pair of these chairs, use 1/16" basswood to make this splat 1/8" in height. Bend it as I suggested for the back. You won't need to glue it with a weight, as the narrowness of this piece will preclude its flattening out.

When you have the chair assembled, it is time to paint it. Although I chose to copy an American chair, I was struck by the Swedish appearance of the unfinished chair. The Swedes' graceful Empire furniture was usually finished in light woods, pale blues, grays, or white. Any of these would be less complicated than the American version.

I painted my chair with golden yellow acrylic, except for the black rectangle on the back. All details were worked out first on a piece of paper, then transferred to the chair by pricking a pin through the design. Use my painting templates as your guide.

Our basic detail is done with a 10/0 brush. Follow the steps in my drawings. For the details, simply place the brush down and lift it up. All of the designs are the same basic brush stroke used in multiples. The black pinstripe edging is

TOOLS AND MATERIALS

- Side Chair kit #40007, House of Miniatures
- 1/16" basswood sheet
- 1/8" basswood strip
- 1/4" balsa sheet
- Two cotton balls
- Cotton twine
- Acrylic paint, yellow and black
- Gold enamel paint
- Craftmark mahogany stain and clear finish
- Tandy Leather punch #102

done with India ink. I used the edge of the cap (see drawing). I tried to paint a smooth thin line with black acrylic but was dissatisfied. I used India ink to cover my mistakes and wondered why I hadn't thought of it first. Be sure the chair is well covered with the yellow paint before you put any India ink on it or it will bleed into the yellow, as I found out. Also be sure to do your stripes one side at a time, letting them dry completely before you do the other side. Try not to handle the ink lines. After you have finished, paint the classical panel on the back in yellow. I tried the pin-prick method, but I couldn't see the marks on the black. I painted the yellow freehand and put gold over it later. It might be better to paint your yellow first, then paint the black around it. Paint the seat black at this time.

Now you are ready to finish the kit. I used Craftmark's clear finish over the entire piece.

Simple, repeated brush strokes make up the designs embellishing the chair above.

The French version of the side chair is very similar to the White House Lincoln era chair.

When this is dry, you may paint the gold detail over the yellow on the back. The gold must be *on top* of the finish. Do not put finish over the gold because it will spread. If I were to do this again I would leave the yellow detail and not paint the gold; this is equally authentic.

Our cushion is a block of basswood 1/8" thick. Use my template for the size. I cut the edges into a sharp point to give it the right shape, put a dab of cotton on top, then glued the fabric as shown in the drawings. Put glue on the edges of the fabric, pull to a point, then clip the fabric as shown. The glue will hold the edges in place.

Glue your cushion to the chair before you add the tassels. If you've done the cushion properly it will be a tight fit. Our tassels are three pieces of cotton twine. Loop them as shown in the drawings, tie a fourth loop in a knot near the top, cut off the excess above the knot, then trim the base. Note: these tassels should be long and hang down front and back (see photograph).

Begin the French style chair with part #12, the sides. Remove the front legs and square the "connection" at the rear legs. Cut 1/16" off the bottom, and narrow the rear legs as shown in the drawing. Taper the inside legs as before.

Our legs are made from Houseworks #7025 balusters. Cut them off at the turning, and then cut them down to just over 1" tall. Reshape the bottoms to make them look like turned feet. Glue them to parts #12.

I made my seat a bit wide. Use the same seat template as for the previous chair. Make the back rail the same way, but the front rail will be deeper and shaped with a swell front, as you see in the photograph. Our cushion is a block of balsa wood, the same size, but shorter. Use 1/4" balsa and shape it to match the swell front. Put a very thin bit of soft cotton ball in the center, then upholster as shown.

I put glue on the inside edges of the fabric, and pulled the edges with the scissors. As you can see from the photographs, you don't need to sew it. I cut the front fabric border from the fabric design and glued it into place. This use of fabric looks much like the original French upholstery. I did not tuck my fabric under; I glued the edge and cut it off with scissors.

Glue the new seat bottom to parts #12. Do not attach the cushion yet.

Our back is cut from a piece of 1/2" basswood 1/16" thick. It is easiest to cut the Gothic arches into your strip of basswood, then go back and cut the back from the strip. This keeps the edges from breaking off. I used a leather punch to make four quatrefoils in the back just above the arches. If you have a small drill, this design would be even nicer if it were cut out.

The French chair has turned front legs. The back is similar to its American counterpart's. The front decoration of the cushion, applied separately, blends perfectly with the remainder of the seat cover.

Our three spindles are toothpicks that I picked up in a restaurant. Plain toothpicks would be almost as nice. You may also substitute Shenandoah Designs #2026 turnings, cut down to size.

The similar Lincoln era chair from the set in the White House has a back almost identical to the French design, except the spindles are plain and set on a raised splat. The openings are between the arches instead of over them. I have included drawings for this Lincoln chair and the leg used on them.

I tried my first rosewood finish on this chair with mixed results. I used a broad, poor quality brush and dry-brush technique. This is great for mahogany finishes, but rosewood needs a crisper line. Use black paint and a fine brush. Stripe the grain around the chair as shown. After you have finished, stain the chair with Craftmark's mahogany finish, followed with clear finish. When it's dry, attach the cushion.

Either of these chairs is a winner. Whichever you choose, you will be adding a bit of history to your house.

Diagrams

All diagrams for this project may be photocopied for personal use

A BLEND OF TWO WHITE HOUSE CHAIRS

taper inside

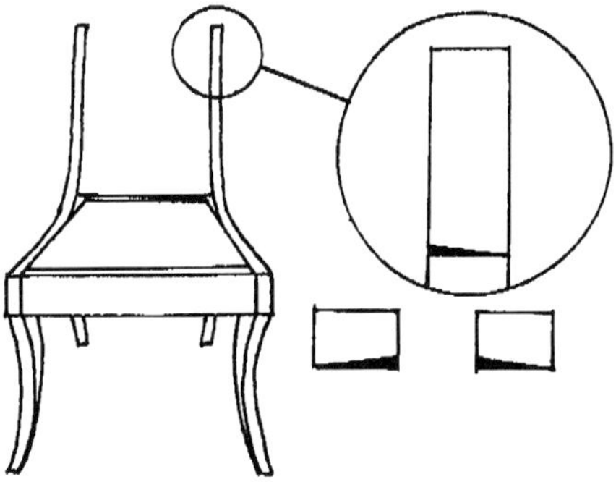

UPRIGHTS, SLIVER REMOVED

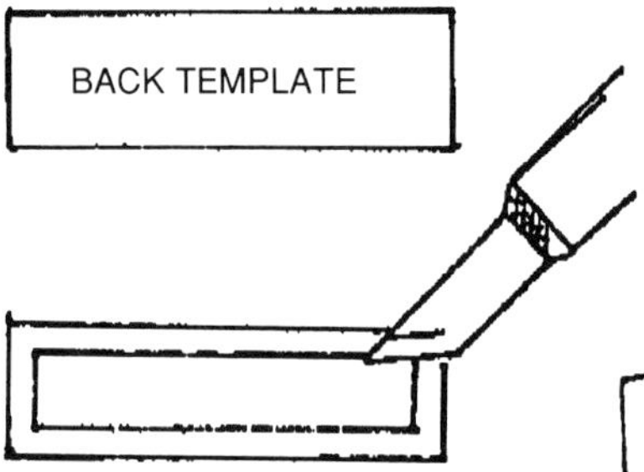

cut paint guidelines

cut splat from extra leg

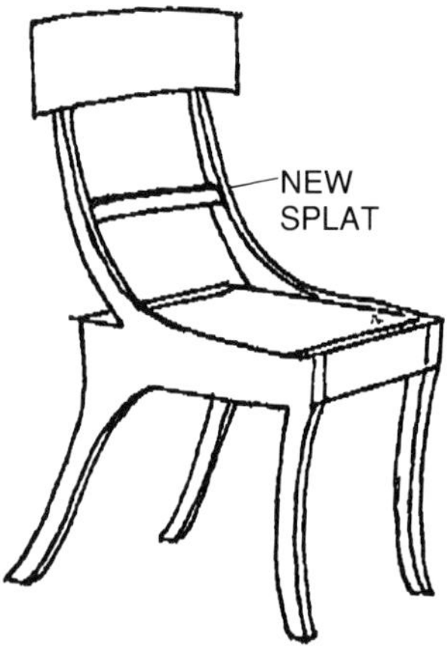

weight to curve back

Diagrams

Kit Renderings

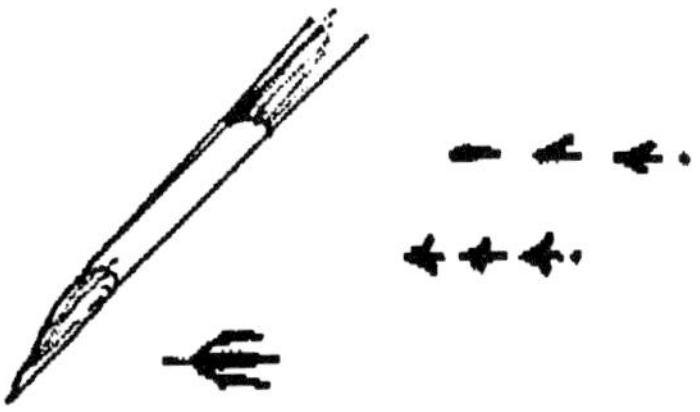

BASIC PAINTING TECHNIQUE

PAINT TEMPLATES

SPLAT

BACK

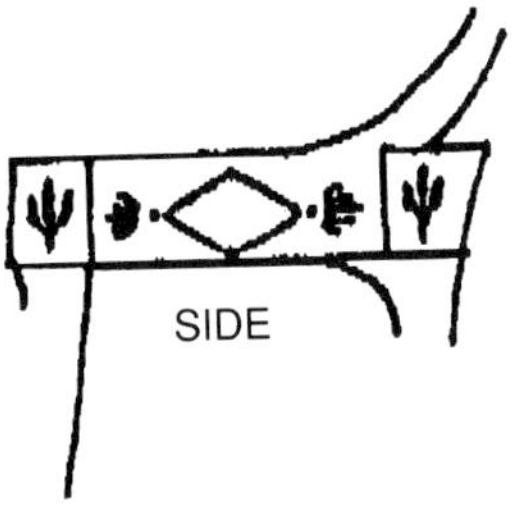

SIDE

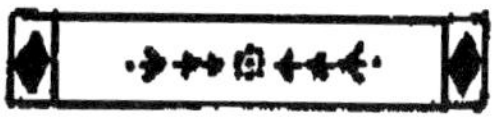

FRONT

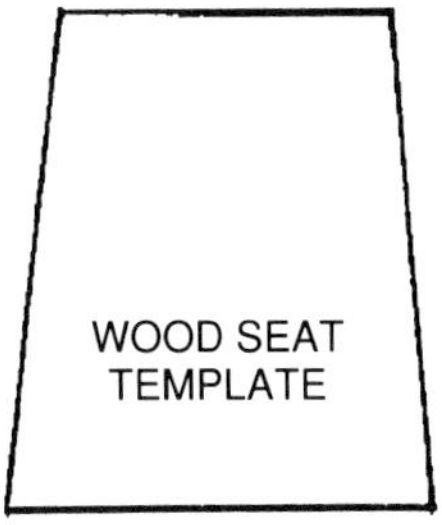

cut angle

WOOD SEAT

ANGLED SEAT

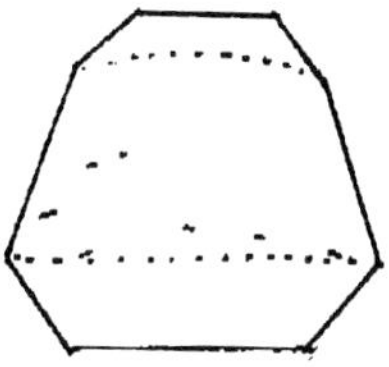

glue front under

place cotton on seat

GLUED FABRIC
front view

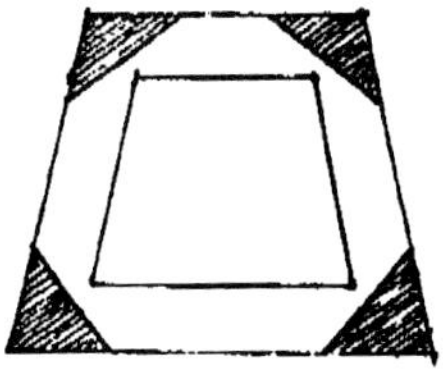

cut fabric as shown

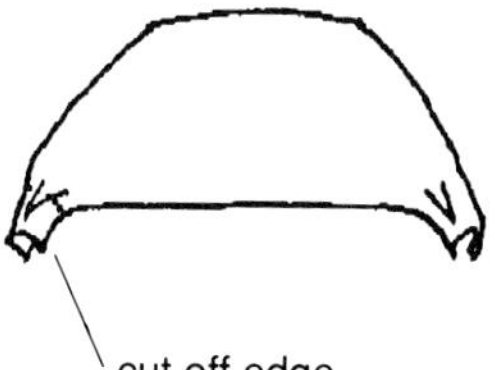

cut off edge

TASSEL CONSTRUCTION

cut 3 strands cotton twine

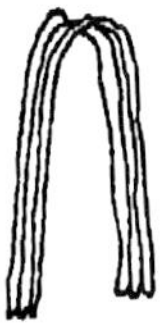

loop over

tie

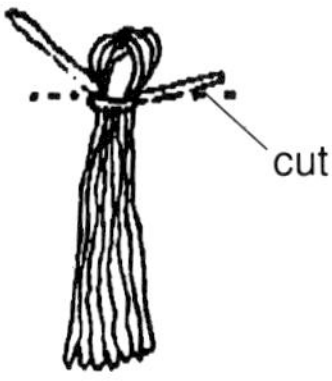

knot

Diagrams

FRENCH VERSION

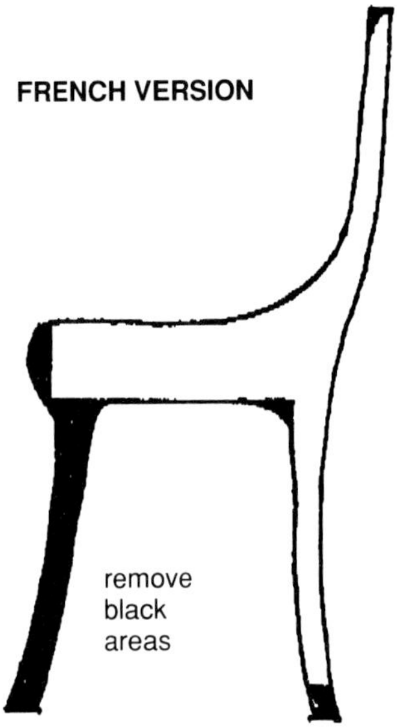

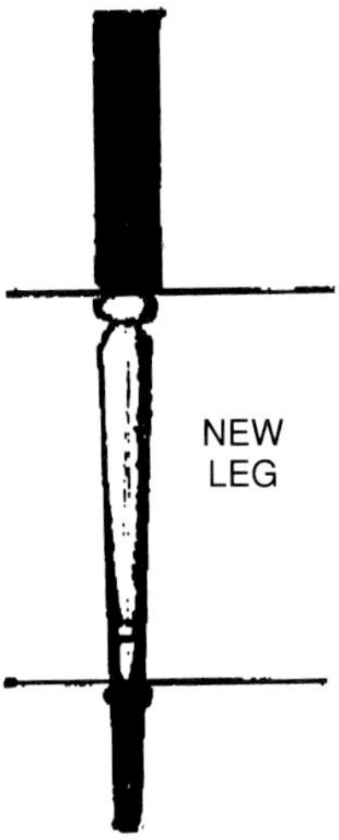

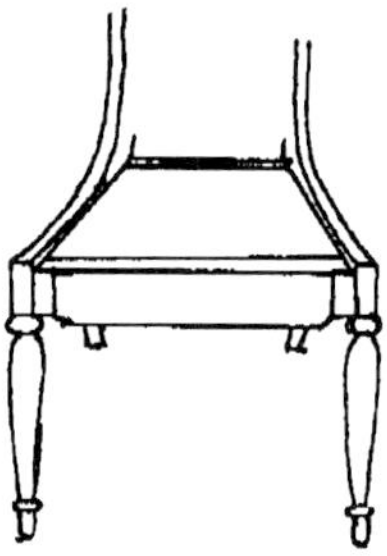

CHAIR FRONT

SHAPED CUSHION

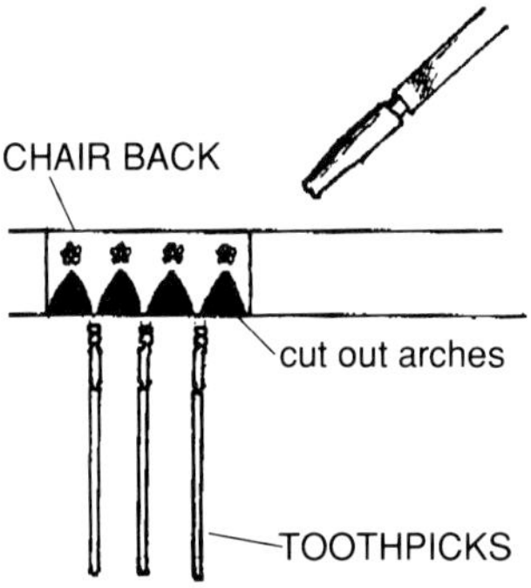

LINCOLN ERA CHAIR

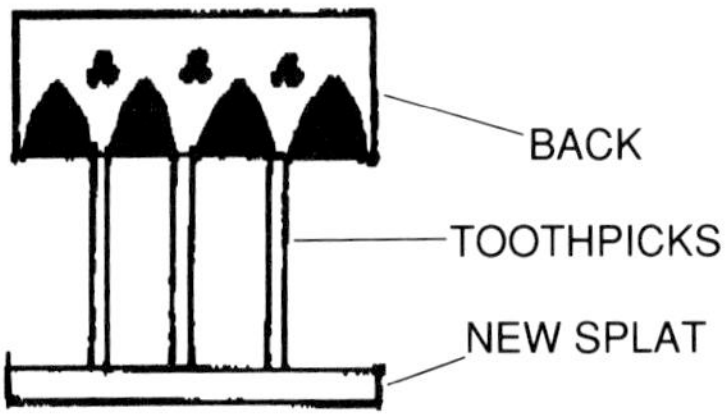

Three in a Bed

A trio of styles repose in this bed

THREE STYLE POSSIBILITIES for the crafter reside in Mini Mundus' #40099 Biedermeier bed (distributed by Miniature Corner) — Empire, Biedermeier, or American. If you make the Empire bed, you will have one of the most elegant pieces of early 19th century furniture. This bed is based on one made for the Empress Josephine in 1805.

The Biedermeier bed would be German or Austrian about 1815. The American sleigh bed is similar to one owned by Washington Irving, which is also identical to one we have in our guest bedroom. Both beds date about 1830. I have chosen to make a beautiful French Empire bed with flecked mahogany finish.

INSTRUCTIONS

Our first alteration is to cut a curved line into the top of part #1, the bedstead. Use the template as a guide. Note that the square molding will be left at an angle when you have cut this line. Square the inside line of this molding as shown in the drawing.

When you have finished this step, slightly round this molding and the matching molding on the footboards, parts #2. It's not incorrect to make the molding half-round, however the visual effect is about the same. Do not glue the headboards in place at this time.

As they come in the kit, the aprons, parts #7, are rather heavy. Our aprons are completely reshaped. Use the template as a guide to reshape them. I cut them with an X-Acto knife, but it would be easier with a small saw. When you have reshaped these, slightly round all the edges except the bottoms (see drawing). This will soften the hard classical lines.

The most difficult alteration is the headboard, part #3. This is difficult because we need to cut two curves into the headboard and still have it look straight. Set up the bed without glue, use "funtack" if needed. Now you can see that a little over 1/8" of the headboards needs to be removed. The exact amount will depend on how much you have removed from the aprons. With a pencil, mark the area to be removed (see drawing). Sand off this excess with a round pencil wrapped in sandpaper. Remove the minimum. Cut the top down and round the top with sandpaper (see drawing).

I eliminated parts #5, the half-round moldings, and substituted 1/8" dowels the same length (see drawing). The dowels are closer to an authentic rail than the molding in the kit.

Except for finishing, the bed is ready to glue together. If you make an Empire bed like mine, you need a rich mahogany finish with ormolu mounts. I used jewelry findings I bought at a show. Hobby and craft shops often sell these in the decoupage section. You may substitute gold paint as well.

Should you decide to do the Biedermeier version, the wood will be light. The gold details will be painted in black to look like inlay. Your library will have many books with both Empire and Biedermeier details to copy.

You may prefer to make an American version. The main change is in the alterations made to the bedstead, parts #1. As you see in the drawing, the upper line is cut in a scallop and the molding is completely eliminated. The base is cut to make legs. This cut is about 5/8" high. Note that the new legs will need to be cut on the inside to match the outside angle (see drawing).

You will need to cut 5/8" off the bottom of the footboards, parts #2 as well, and to eliminate the molding. The remainder of the instructions will stay the same. There is no ormolu nor inlay, and the mahogany will not be the same type as in the French bed.

The French bed is finished in simulated flecked mahogany, a rare freak grain preferred by French cabinetmakers. First wipe Craftmark's mahogany finish thinly over all exposed parts. This will give a very light mahogany finish. When this is dry, swirl a second coat on with tiny circular motions (see drawing). This is quite tedious, but gives a beautiful effect. Let this dry; then using a square tipped brush, dry brush black water-based paint lightly over the entire finish (see drawing). You may want to try this on a sample before you do it on your bed. Your brush should be very dry. When the black wash is dry, use a small natural sponge to deepen the burl effect with Jamestown Colony red paint. Be sure your sponge is almost dry. Dab it all over the exposed wood until you get the desired effect. Finish with Craftmark's clear finish.

I put the "ormolu" on with wood glue, which I let become almost dry on a spare piece of cardboard. I used a toothpick to put the glue on and nudge the "ormolu" into place. These beds are displayed with one side against the wall, therefore the ormolu or inlay is on one side only. Do not put these decorations on both sides.

Our American version of this bed is done with Craftmark's mahogany finish swirled on in the pattern shown in the drawing. This is done on both sides, but the ends are plain mahogany, not fancy.

I raised the height of the mattress just over 1/8". This should be done for all three versions. These were tall beds. I glued 1/8" strips of basswood to a piece of matboard or thin basswood, and then I glued the mattress on top of that. The bedspread is glued into place as shown in the drawing.

The bolsters are shortened pencils or dowels wrapped in thin plastic foam, that spongy "paper" we have used before. I used masking tape to help them hold their shape, then I upholstered over the edge (see drawing). I suggest you glue the bolsters in place on top of the bedspread, one at each end.

Should you put one of these beds in your miniature home, be sure your owners are not tall. Since the boards at both ends are identical in height, it pays to have a single guest, or a short couple. Whichever you choose, you'll never be short on compliments.

TOOLS AND MATERIALS

- Mini Mundus #40099 Biedermeier Bed
- X-Acto knife
- Craftmark mahogany stain
- Craftmark clear finish
- Black water-based paint
- Minicolor Jamestown Colony Red water based paint
- Flat stiff brush
- Jewelry findings (optional)
- Gold paint (optional)
- Two short pencils or similar size dowels
- Foam wrap
- Thin fabric for upholstery
- Matboard or thin basswood
- 1/8" sq basswood strip
- 1/8" dowel

Diagrams

Kit Renderings

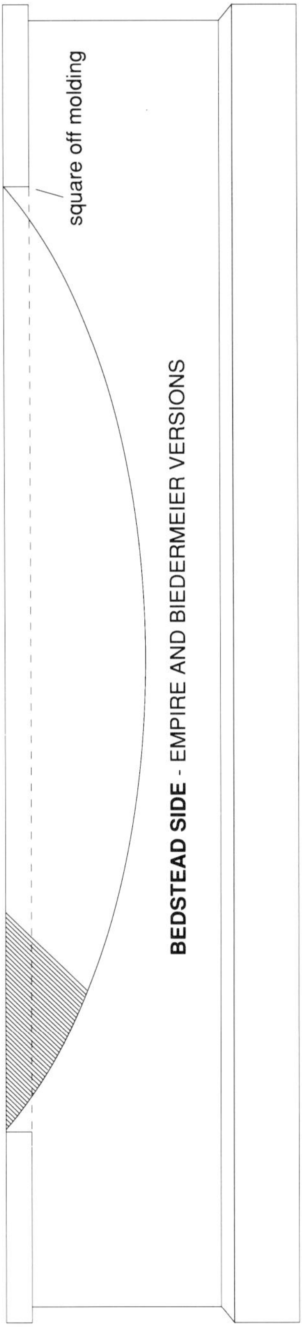

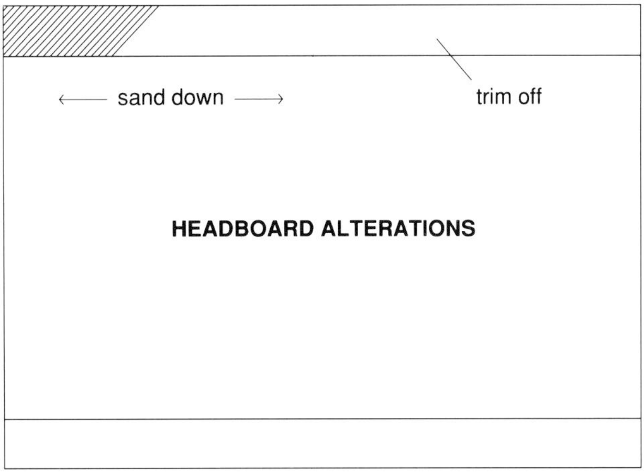

HEADBOARD
side view

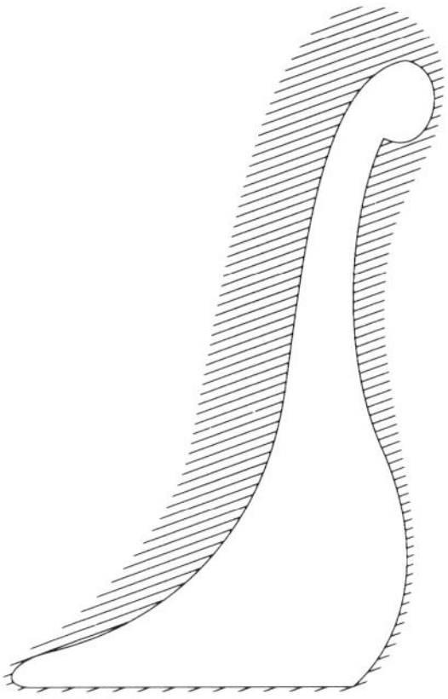

APRON RESHAPED

round apron edge

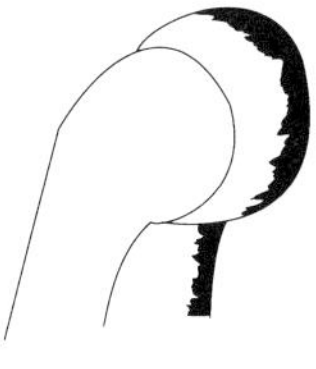

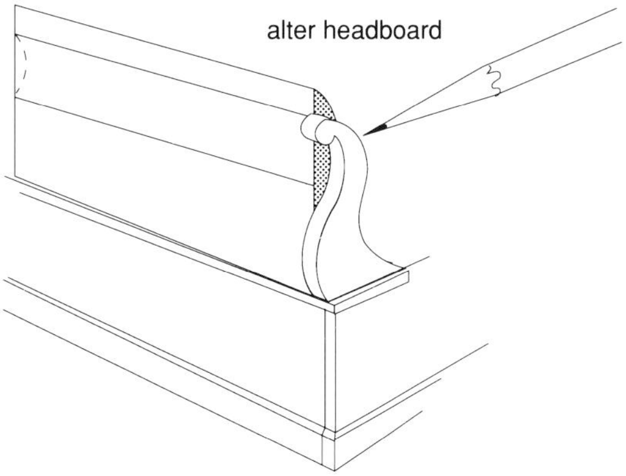

Diagrams

Kit Renderings

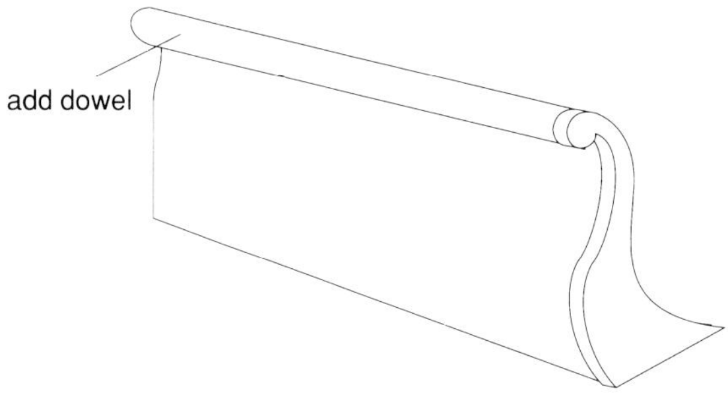

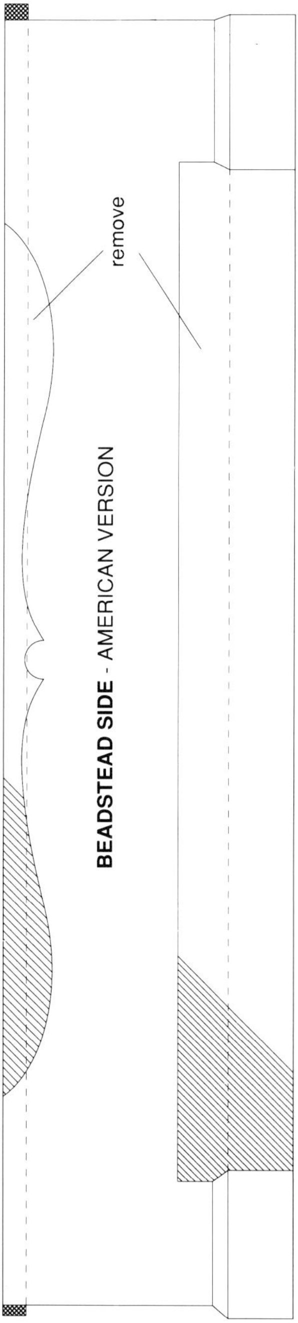

EMPIRE FINISH STEPS

Coat thinly with mahogany finish; let dry, then . . .

1 - swirl with mahogany finish

2 - dry brush black paint

3 - sponge on red color

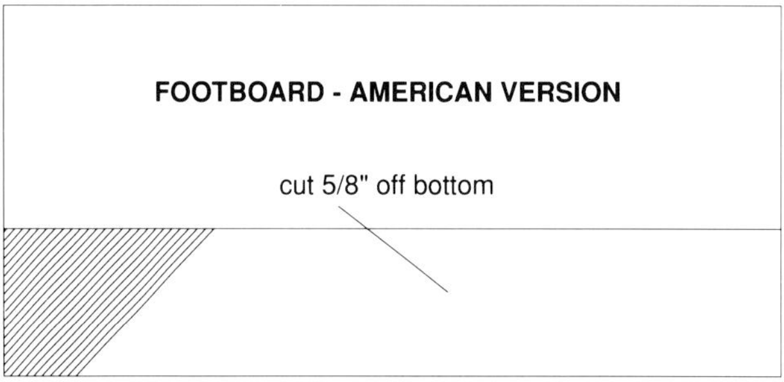

Diagrams

Kit Renderings

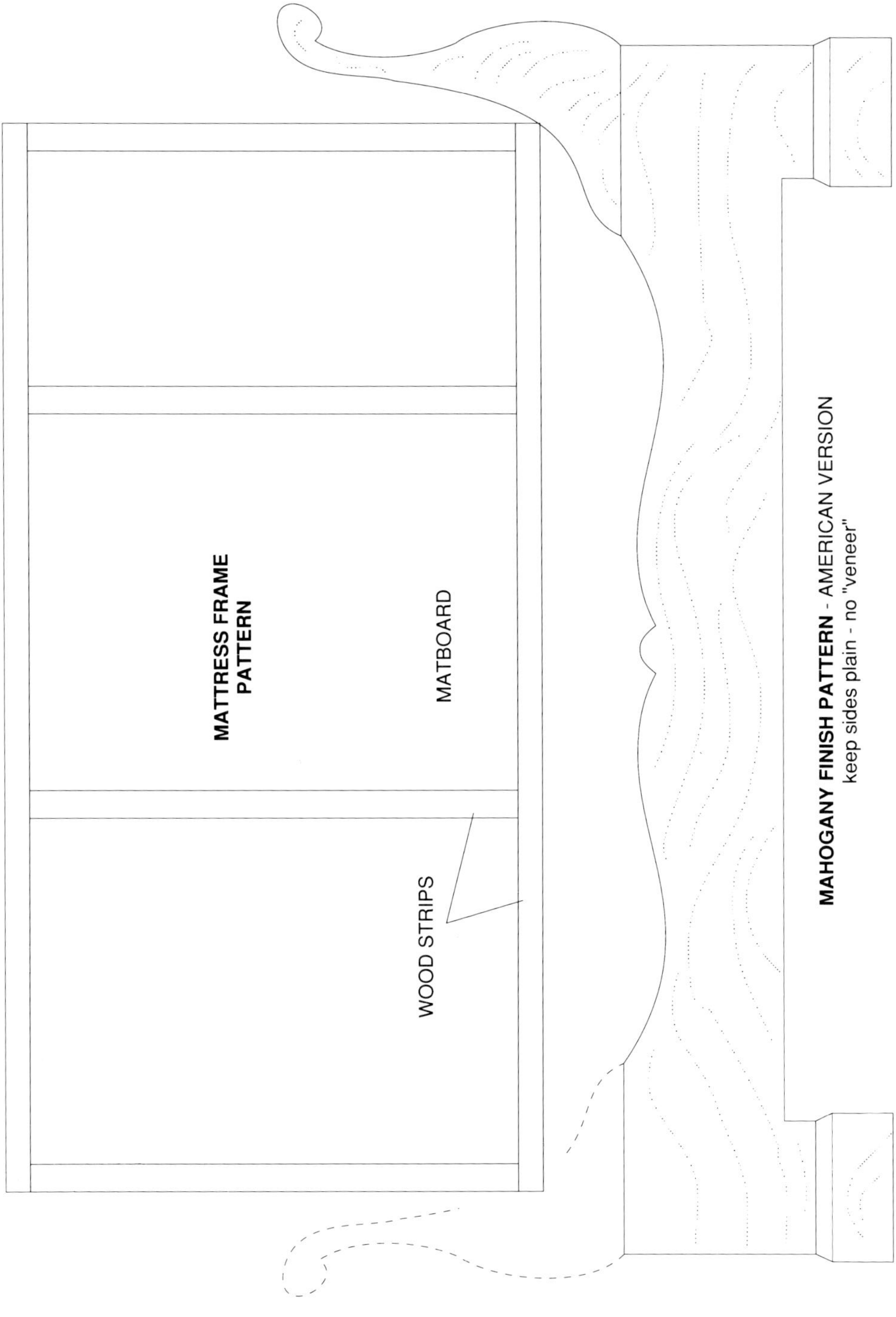

Diagrams

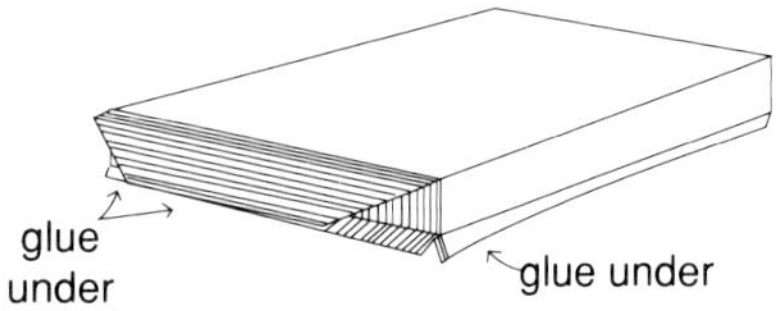

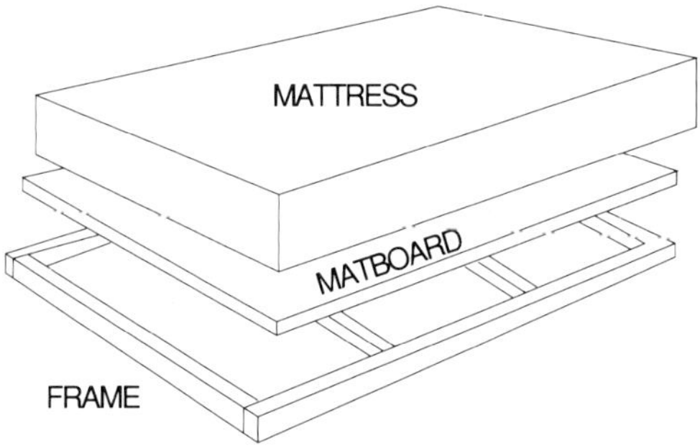

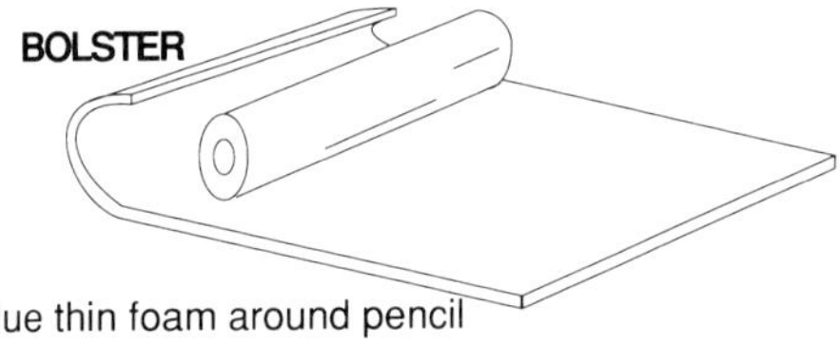

glue thin foam around pencil

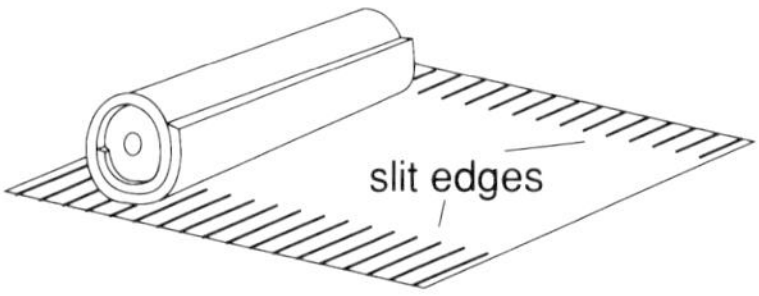

glue fabric around bolster

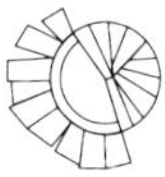

glue end strips
on each other

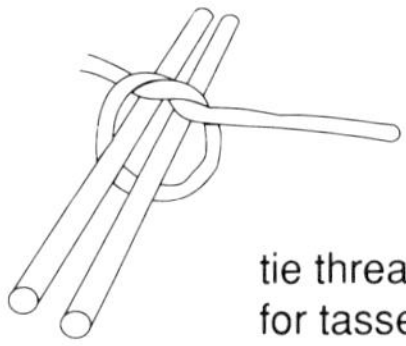

tie threads
for tassel;
trim ends even